Haunting & History
of the
Battle of Gettysburg

A Collection of Paranormal Photographs
and Experiences from the Gettysburg
Battlefield with Historical Narrative.

By Barry Strohm

Acknowledgements

After 46 years of married life, my wife, Connie thought she had heard it all. Then she heard me say "I think I will write a book." Coming from someone that got straight "D"s in all his college English courses, she had to think I had finally flipped out for sure. When she realized it would be about the Battle of Gettysburg, she became almost coherent. After all, one of our first dates 50 years ago was a visit to the Gettysburg Battlefield. When she realized it was about the paranormal, I almost lost her again. Without her help and support this book would never been possible. Our life together has been a true adventure and I have given new meaning to "what would you like to be when you grow up." There is no one with whom I would rather have shared the adventure.

Steve McNaughton, author of *Ghostly Connections* and *Pennsylvania's Adams County Ghosts*, taught me how to understand and investigate the presence of spirits. Steve was the founder of the P.E.E.R. investigative group and owner of the Chestnut Hall Bed and Breakfast here in New Oxford. Without Steve's help, this book would not have become a reality.

Finally, I would like to give my thanks to my clairvoyant friend, Barbara Lee Rowe. She never ceases to amaze me with names and facts that research proves to be correct. There are multiple stories in this book of her remarkable abilities. She shares my passion to memorialize the spirits of the brave soldiers that fought on the hallowed ground of Gettysburg. Barbara Lee currently assists me with ghost tours at Golden Lane Art and Antique Gallery in which live communications with the spirit world has brought comfort to the tour guests. She is truly a remarkable person!

Contents

INTRODUCTION

Spirits, Orbs and the Paranormal

T HE town of Gettysburg and its surrounding area is one of the most haunted areas in the Country. In 1863 almost 150,000 fighting men of the Blue and the Gray collided in three of the most violent days in American military history. This volume will present a collection of paranormal photography dedicated to honoring the spirits of the fallen that still remain. Accompanying the pictures will be a short history outlining the events that influenced the continuing paranormal activity. Whatever your beliefs, the pictures will challenge your imagination for so called scientific explanations.

An appropriate starting place for a discussion of paranormal abnormalities is the appearance of orbs. There are many individuals that claim the existence of orbs in photographs is easily explained as dust or pollen reflecting the light for the camera. After viewing the images in this book, you might agree that not all orbs can be as easily explained. Orbs are round in shape, often have inner bands, a diffused outer edge and capable of moving at very high rates of speed. While not a part of this book, I have video clips showing actual orb movements that can be viewed in slow motion that include interactions with humans. I believe that this speed of movement is a reason why most individuals have never realized contact with the spirit world. If you are taking a picture with a flash camera, there is a lot of luck involved in getting a picture of an orb that is moving rapidly and you cannot see it visually.

In most instances I personally am unable to see the orbs, as I am not sensitive, like a medium, to the presence of spirits. Usually I observe the screen in the back of the cameras for activity. Sometimes light will reflect off the orbs when I use the flash on my cameras. One night while photographing on the Wheatfield near the New York artillery monument, I was aware of a streak of light while taking a picture. When I looked at the pictures on the computer that night I witnessed the picture on the following page.

As previously mentioned, orbs move at a very high rate of speed. In the image above, an orb can be seen moving rapidly through the picture over the cannon on the right. It moved that distance, approximately 20 feet, in 1/60th of a second, the period of time the lens of the camera was open. Other orbs in the image are stationary including one on the left cannon.

The actual composition of an orb is a mystery. I believe that it is a representation of the spirit energy or soul of an individual, either human or animal. They inhabit a dimension of which we know little. In many instances, a close up of an orb in a picture will show the features of the individual or animal as it was in life or at time of death. There will be many instances of such images in this book. Skeptics of the paranormal will postulate pages upon pages of pseudo scientific reasons why orbs are simply reflections of dust, water or whatever. They will state that images in the orbs are the product of an over active imagination or finger prints on the lens of the camera. While many orbs are easily explained, this volume will show examples of orbs in the image of departed soldiers and even mascots of the North and South that will challenge conventional explanation. If orbs were dust or pollen, their appearance from one photograph to another taken from the same spot in rapid sequence would be similar. Orbs actually change size, color and shape quite rapidly.

Let's pursue the dust and pollen argument. The month of February, 2010 saw multiple blizzards in the Gettysburg area. Having never attempted to photograph paranormal abnormalities after a snow storm, I loaded up my cameras and headed for the battlefield in 20 degree tem-

peratures on a clear, still night. I can assure you that there was no dust or pollen in the air that night. In the picture above you will see an image showing the Indiana Volunteers monument near Spangler Spring with snow and orbs. Apparently the temperature did not affect the orbs as much as it affected my shivering. I was very happy for image stabilization feature on my camera.

In the picture below, taken along the Cemetery Ridge defensive line, an orb changes from neon blue to a light emitting form. The pictures were taken approximately 2 seconds apart on separate hand held cameras.

I have photographed orbs in many different colors and sizes. There is no definitive proof of the significance of the different colors.

Pictured here is a bright green neon orb that was photographed at the Triangular Field. Note the facial image in the lower part of the orb. This shade of green is rarely seen.

This neon red orb was photographed on Seminary Ridge where the Army of Northern Virginia positioned their cannon for the grand barrage. I have no idea of the significance of the different colors seen in orb photography.

Many photographs of orbs have facial images. In my opinion you are looking at the images of individuals that passed in the service of their countries almost 150 years ago.

Throughout the book you will see images of orbs that are quite large in size. Pictured on the top of the next page are two large orbs photographed at the Angle. The monument is a good reference point to estimate the size of the orbs.

Orbs can take on the appearance of a shooting comet as they move rapidly and emit light. Recorded on Seminary Ridge, this orb seems to be avoiding the tree limbs as it quickly moves through the area.

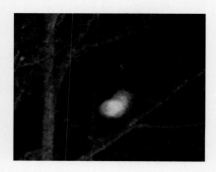

Spirit orbs take many forms and colors on the battlefield, from neon blue to red, yellow, white and many color variations. The image below of the 148th Pennsylvania Volunteers monument was recorded at the wheatfield. This is a very unusual combination of colored orbs in a single photo. The yellow one on the right has a very unusual pattern.

The Celtic Cross marks the spot where the Irish Brigade fought on the second day of the battle. The Irish Wolf Hound on the monument signifies loyalty. This image was included to show the orb which seems to be emitting light that is reflecting on the monument. It also seems to be protecting the Wolf Hound. This is an area of very agressive paranormal activity which is cover in later chapters.

In the photograph on the next page, taken near Iverson's Pits, the edge of an orb field is readily apparent. It also shows a wide variety of colors in the orbs, especially the orange one on the right side of the picture. Most importantly, the left side of the image is clear of any orbs. If it were dust, pollen, or any other objects reflecting light they would be across the entire photo. This is the only time I have been able to photograph the edge of an orb field. In my experience, orbs often tend to travel in large groups. In many instances, the first picture taken with flash will have a group of orbs and the next picture will be free of any paranormal activity.

I believe that the orbs on these pages are not specks of dust or pollen. Others will say that the images are the result of fingerprints or dirt on the camera lens. I can assure you my lenses are clean when I take the pictures.

The next page is a collage of orbs with the images of faces in them. Skeptics would say they are like ink spots and your imagination reminds you of some type of facial image. Others will say they are created by finger prints on the lenses. I propose that you will see orbs containing the faces of the soldiers that fought and gave their lives at Gettysburg. Some of the faces are more distinct than others. All of the images will test the fingerprint on the lens theory. I also included a

This light emitting orb was taken on a humid night in the Slaughter Pen looking toward Little Round Top. As seen in the light trail behind the orb, it was traveling at a very high rate of speed. My lens was open only 1/60th of a second. Orbs appear in all sizes, shapes and colors and quite often at a very high rate of speed.

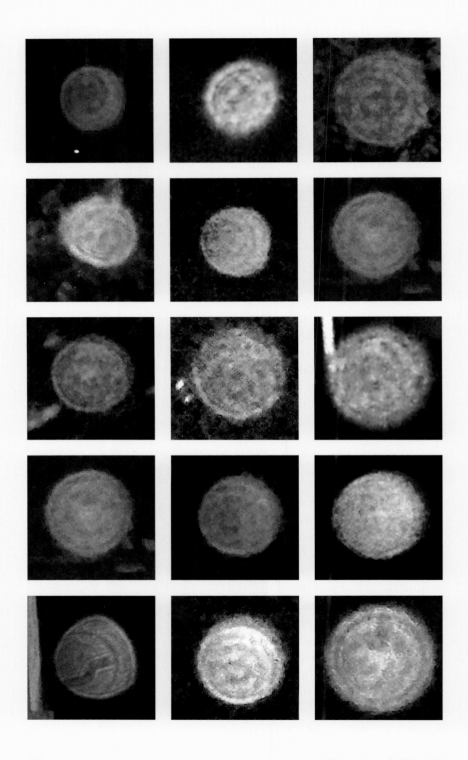

couple of animal faces in orbs to test your imagination. As you look at the faces you are staring into a dimension of which we can only speculate, but they are in all probability of another century and time. I have many more similar images in my files.

In this chapter I have attempted to create a compelling argument for the association of orbs with the human spirit or soul. As you view the numerous photographs in this book, feel free to suggest an explanation other than paranormal activity.

In a photograph taken in Rose's Woods, a very unusual orb seems to be watching me from behind a tree limb. I thought it was a bit unusual that the tree limb did not throw a shadow on the orb. The spirits act as they did in life, taking cover behind the protection of a tree or other object.

This vividly colored orb with a facial image was photographed in Devil's Den.

Chapter One

The Stage is Set

In the early 1860s, the weapons of war were becoming much more efficient at taking lives than military tactics were at preserving them. Smoothbore muzzle loading rifles were accurate to 100 yards. Rifled muskets, now the infantry weapon of choice, were accurate at 300 yards and beyond. Special units of trained sharpshooters were able to kill at 600 yards. Breech loading weapons such as the Smith and Sharps Carbine would double the rate of fire from that of muzzle loaders. The Spencer Repeating Rifle, developed by the Union, had a 7 cartridge tube in the stock that allowed true rapid fire at as many as 20 rounds per minute from a hand held weapon. Two regiments of Custer's Michigan Brigade carried Spencer Carbines in the engagement at Gettysburg's East Cavalry field.

Artillery, the long arm of the armies, was also undergoing radical change. Smoothbore cannon fired round shot that lost velocity rapidly and acted like a bowling ball as it bounced along the ground. A 10-pdr. Napoleon cannon, used by both sides at the beginning of the war, had a maximum range of 1,550 yards with solid rounds. Cased shot fired from the Napoleon was accurate to 600 yards and canister to 300 yards. These rounds made the smoothbore cannon highly effective against massed infantry, as Pickett's Division would find out on July 3rd. A 3-inch Parrot rifled cannon was capable of firing a projectile 2,000 yards with far greater accuracy than the smooth bore guns. The famous "Swamp Angel" that bombarded Charleston in 1863 fired a 200 lb. projectile from 7,000 yards. Hollow shells were filled with black powder and ignited by a fuse timed to explode over the heads of the enemy sending shrapnel in all directions. By 1863, both sides used the rifled cannon for long range and smoothbore artillery for close range support of infantry. Both North and South had the utensils of war capable of inflicting horrific casualties.

By late June of 1863 forces were in play that would soon make the sleepy village of Gettysburg, population around 2,400, the scene of the most violent military clash to take place in the United States. In early May, General Lee had won an overwhelming victory at Chancellorsville in spite of being vastly outnumbered. He had once again shown that he was a far better general than the best of the Army of the Potomac, especially the bumbling Joe Hooker. A feeling of invincibility swept the Army as well as the commanders of the Army of Northern Virginia. Morale of the southern troops had never been greater than in June 1863.

Unfortunately for the Confederacy, the recent death of Stonewall Jackson, shot by his own men at the battle of Chancellorsville, had taken the best fighting corps commander from the Southern army. This loss had far reaching implications that would have a profound effect on the upcoming invasion of the North. Lee was forced to reorganize the structure of the Army of Northern Virginia. He now had three Army Corps, commanded by General Longstreet, General Ewell and General A. P. Hill. Two of his three generals had no experience as corp commanders. Both Ewell and Hill would make questionable command decisions that had a negative effect on the outcome of the battle and shaped the destiny of the entire Confederacy. There were also inexperienced Generals promoted to command at the division level. The death of Jackson would truly have a far reaching effect in ways never anticipated by General Lee or Jefferson Davis.

Vicksburg, Miss., the Confederate fortress of the West, was about to fall to General Ulysses S. Grant. Losing Vicksburg would split the Southern States in two. General Lee and President Jefferson Davis decided on an invasion of the North that would hopefully bring a swift end to the war. Lee also knew that the South was losing its' ability to provide ammunition and supplies and the summer of 1863 was the last opportunity for a sustained attack above the Mason Dixon Line. A southern victory could allow England to intervene on the side of the South and break the cotton blockade.

As the invasion began, General Lee had his calvary under J.E.B. Stuart raiding as far north as Carlisle, PA in an attempt to gain much needed supplies and weaken Northern resolve. Stuart was to keep in communication with General Lee and inform him if Northern troops were on the move or concentrating in any one area. Unfortunately for the Southern army, this did not happen and lack of knowledge concerning the location of the Army of the Potomac may be the main reason for the loss at Gettysburg.

General Lee also failed to realize the amount of Federal artillery that could be moved to the Gettysburg area in a short period of time. At the height of the battle, 372 pieces of Federal artillery in 67 batteries were present and well positioned under the experienced command of General Henry Hunt. These units had adequate ammunition in reserve to efficiently fight the battle.

The Confederates had 283 cannon present to support their operations. Poor command decisions kept many of their guns in reserve and out of use during critical times of the battle. Additionally, the Confederates were plagued with shortages of ammunition, and what they did have was of poor quality, especially the fuses that timed the explosions of the shells. The poor quality of fuses contributed to the ineffectiveness of the barrage prior to Pickett's charge, as many of the shells exploded to the rear of the Union defensive line.

As part of the initial advance, General Early moved his Division as far east as York, PA and threatened to capture Harrisburg, panicking the local population. Union militia actually burned the bridge in Wrightsville, a small town east of York on the Susquehanna River, to stop the threatened advance. As Ewell's Corp threatened Harrisburg, Lee had maneuvered his remaining two Corps north into Central Pennsylvania and was located in the vicinity of the town of Chambersburg. When all of his troops were concentrated, Lee's war machine numbered 75,000 men.

This was the first time Southern troops, the majority of which came from Virginia, were on Northern soil and it was "get even" time. The State of Virginia had been devastated by war for nearly two years and it was time for the abolitionist in the North to get a taste of their own medicine. In spite of orders to the contrary, rebel soldiers robbed homes and destroyed properties along the invasion route. Black residents were fleeing for their lives. Confederate troops were rounding up anyone of African descent, whether runaway slave or a free man for generations. They were sent back to slavery below the Mason Dixon Line. This was truly the time to pay back the abolitionists of the North for the devastation of Virginia and not allowing the Southern States to succeed from the Union. Any supplies, wagons, food or horses were confiscated by the foraging Rebel forces.

Lee told his Generals that he intended to force the Army of the Potomac to attack him and fight a defensive battle on the terrain of his choosing. He gave specific orders to his Generals not to engage the Union Army without his approval. If the Army of Northern Virginia was to be successful they must fight from "good" ground of their own choosing. His Generals, especially First Corp Commander Longstreet, were very much in agreement about the strategy to fight a defensive battle. The loss of the high ground in Gettysburg became a major factor leading to the ultimate Southern defeat.

In contrast to the high morale and the feeling of invincibility on the part of the Rebels, morale in the Union army reached a low point after the defeats of Fredericksburg and Chancellorsville. Poor command decisions from Federal Generals had once again squandered victory and caused heavy loss of life. The citizens of the Union were in a state of panic that Rebel Armies were on Northern soil. President Lincoln's popularity was at an all time low and his reelection looked doubtful. The President had grown impatient with General Joe Hooker after his recent humiliating defeat at Chancellorsville and offered the command to General John Reynolds, the popular Commander of the First Corps. Reynolds turned down the offer, preferring to remain in a fighting command. This decision ultimately cost him his life, as he was one of the first to fall at Gettysburg, victim of a sharpshooters' bullet. As news of the Rebel invasion spread, the Army of the Potomac was situated in a rough line from Frederick, MD to central Pennsylvania. Hooker once again could not make definitive decisions concerning either the size of the Confederate invasion or how to defeat it.

Hooker offered his letter of resignation in a dispute over whether the soldiers stationed at Harpers Ferry should be transferred to the Army of the Potomac and become part of the troops defending against the invasion. To the General's surprise, Lincoln accepted his resignation. The President replaced General Hooker with George Meade as Commander of the 100,000 man Army of the Potomac. Meade was a topographical engineer and regarded as a competent military leader. Lincoln gave Meade the orders to defend Washington DC and the cities of Pennsylvania. General Meade was given command on June 28, only 3 days before the Battle and did not have time to solidify his staff or chain of Command.

Meade ordered three corps of the Army of the Potomac to position themselves in a northeast direction between York, PA and Manchester, MD. Reynolds, Howard and Sickles were ordered to stand between Emmitsburg and Taneytown. Unknown to the Rebel commanders who were without cavalry support, the entire Army of the Potomac was within marching distance of the town of Gettysburg. Meade also devised a fall back defensive line along the Pipe Creek valley in the event that the invading Confederates were not defeated in the initial contact.

For almost two years the Army of the Potomac was stationed in the enemy territory of Virginia. They were cursed at, shot by "bushwackers" and forced to stay in guarded camps for their own protection. In addition, they had suffered defeat after defeat because of inept decisions by their Generals. With each step northward they were getting closer to the support of the citizens of the Union. The morale of the Union Army increased with every step as they moved into Northern territory. As they marched, the soldiers were now met with cheers, food and water. They actually celebrated as their units crossed the Mason Dixon Line. Now they were defending their own homes! This change in morale became a major factor as the Federal troops would face the invaders with courage and bravery.

The die was cast for a horrific military engagement in which almost one in three of the men involved was to become a casualty of war, from high ranking Generals to privates of infantry, drummer boys and even canine mascots. No one really knows how many casualties occurred at the battle. Union records are fairly accurate but the Confederate records are not nearly as detailed because much of the command structure was killed. In addition, many of the Rebel dead were buried by their own comrades and no record was made of the location of the quickly dug graves. In some instances, the Rebel reports intentionally understated the casualties so as to not alarm the citizens of the South. It is truly a shame that the understating of casualties is the only history lesson learned by our modern Presidents.

Approximately 52,000 men were killed, wounded or captured in a period of only 3 days. About 3,200 Union soldiers and 3,500 Confederate soldiers were listed as killed. Around 14,500 Union troops and 15,250 Rebel troops were wounded, of which approximately 20% succumbed to their injuries or disease. Many that survived had debilitating injuries that affected them for the rest of their lives. The US Provost Marshall reported that there were 5,425 unwounded and 6,802 wounded Confederate prisoners taken at Gettysburg. Of those captured, as many as 25% did not survive the ordeal of living in a prisoner of war camp. I personally found it hard to comprehend the scope of the carnage of Gettysburg. Beaver Stadium at Penn State University holds 107,000 people. Think of ½ the people attending a Penn State game as being a casualty of war.

A huge burden was placed upon the 2,400 citizens of the town of Gettysburg. The task of caring for the wounded of both sides, possibly as many as 30,000 individuals, as well as burying the dead under a hot

July sun would fall to these residents. There was no powered equipment to help dig the graves in 1863. Over 5,000 horses were killed with their bodies requiring disposal. Most of the animals were drenched with kerosene and set afire, creating an unbelievable stench. Confederate bodies were buried in mass graves near where they fell. As a result of monies raised by charities in the South, many of the Rebel bodies were re-interred between 1871 and 1873 to cemeteries in North and South Carolina as well as Virginia. The Hollywood Cemetery in Richmond has a special area set aside for the bodies of those killed in Gettysburg. Records show that 3,250 bodies were removed to the South but over 3,500 southern soldiers were killed; meaning that the bodies of many soldiers were never recovered and still remain in the hallowed ground of Gettysburg. Perhaps these bodies contribute to the vast paranormal activities found in the area of the battle field.

The bodies of identified Federal soldiers were sent home for burial by their families. Most were placed in temporary graves for later reburial. Many of the unidentified soldiers were later re-buried in the new National Cemetery that became the site of Lincoln's famous Gettysburg Address on Nov. 19, 1863. By March 1864 when burial operations were completed, 3,512 Union soldiers were buried in the cemetery; of these, 979 are unknown.

S.G. Elliot, an engineer, prepared a map shortly after the battle that showed the location of mass grave sites. Fallen soldiers buried by the Confederates would not be shown on the map. This source was instrumental when the fallen southern troops were disinterred as much as 30 years after the battle. The map is also useful in showing areas of paranormal activity. Taverns, homes and churches were turned into temporary hospitals where dead bodies were literally stacked to the ceiling, floors stained with blood that can be seen today. Bodies and body parts from amputations were buried in front yards and gardens. The smell of death permeated the air to the extent that the residents were forced to cover their noses with handkerchiefs soaked in perfume. Citizens as far away as Harrisburg could smell the odor of death. The stench hung in the air until the cold temperatures of winter froze the rotting flesh.

It is impossible to understand the true horror of the aftermath of the battle. During the fighting, many fences were torn down allowing livestock to escape. One account describes the impact of groups of wild swine feeding on bodies of the dead. A wounded soldier immobilized on the Wheatfield fought off a group of the pigs with his saber all night until he was rescued by the ambulance corps in the morning.

The human suffering and death at Gettysburg sets the stage for unparalleled paranormal abnormalities and haunting. Having grown up near Gettysburg I was always fascinated by the history of the battle and became increasingly aware of the incredible and often unbelievable paranormal activity associated with the area. In this work, I will explain a brief historical overview of the applicable segment of the battle and show actual photographs of paranormal activity that I have taken at the specific area. All photographs are real and represent the best of over 50,000 images and many hours on the battlefield at night, mostly by myself. While most of my encounters have been friendly and enlightening, there have been times that I felt real fear.

My equipment consists of three 12.1 megapixel digital cameras mounted on a metal strip so I can take rapid sequence photos with flash. On most evenings I take as many as 700 pictures. I also carry a very powerful flash light. In most instances I am photographing shadow images at night using flash lighting. Often the images are small and require enlarging to see the detail, resulting in a grainy picture. I hope the subject matter will more than compensate for occasional lack of quality in the photographs.

Dealing with the paranormal is an encounter with the unexpected. Included will be photographs that will test your imagination and several in which I have no clue as to their cause. There will also be several personal encounters and stories in association with a local medium. Whether you believe in an individual's ability to communicate with spirits or not, I have seen her provide names and facts, with no prior knowledge, that research has proven to be true. You may find her contributions to this book hard to believe, but they happened in front of other witnesses.

I did not believe in the paranormal for the first 60 years of my life and I certainly never believed I would be writing a book on the spirit world. Whatever your beliefs, my collection of photographs will challenge the way in which you look at the afterlife in the future. The opinions given in this book are strictly my own and I want you to make up your own minds. I can assure the reader that everything in this book is real and the paranormal experiences factual.   My goal has been to treat the happenings with awe and respect for the unbelievably brave men that shed their blood on the soil of a town named Gettysburg and whose spirits remain to assure that we never forget.

Chapter Two

The Beginning of the Storm

THE conflict actually began on June 30 when a Confederate column under Brigadier General James J. Pettigrew approached Gettysburg on the Chambersburg Road (US. Rt. 30 today), supposedly looking for supplies and shoes. Halting his men outside the town, the General rode to Seminary Ridge and observed a large column of Union troops approaching the town from the South on the Emmitsburg Pike (currently Bus. Rt.15). The General believed the Union column was local militia that would be no match for his battle tried veterans. Respecting the strict orders by General Lee not to engage with Union forces, he reversed his column and marched west to the town of Cashtown, approximately 7 miles from Gettysburg. Upon reaching Cashtown, he reported to his Corp Commander, General A. P. Hill. General Lee had not yet arrived, as he was in the town of Chambersburg with First Corp Commander, General Longstreet. Southern cavalry, the eyes of the army under the command of J.E.B. Stuart, was also absent, leaving the Rebel Generals with no definitive knowledge of the location of the Army of the Potomac.

The column observed by General Pettigrew was actually two Brigades of veteran Federal cavalry, commanded by General John Buford, moving north from the Frederick, MD area. His troops were attempting to confirm the exact location of the southern invaders. Buford was a native of Kentucky and graduated from West Point. In spite of being southern by birth he chose to fight with the Federal Army. His Division was the same force that handed Stuart and the famed southern cavalry their first defeat at Brandy Station several weeks earlier. Having observed the Rebel column heading east on the Chambersburg Pike, General Buford sent a dispatch to General John Reynolds, commander of the Union First Corps, that he intended to resist any Southern advance toward the town of Gettysburg with his approximately 2,700 men.

General Reynolds replied that he would march with his entire First Corps to support Buford's cavalry at first light.

General Buford, well aware that he did not have the manpower to hold the Rebels, decided that he would fight a "Defense in Depth." Under this strategy, his men would fight a delaying action while falling back to a main line of defense. In this case his main line of defense was McPherson Ridge, a knoll of high ground situated about 2 miles from Gettysburg. His hope was to delay the Confederates until the First Corps could reinforce the McPherson Ridge position. Buford's men fought like infantry behind hastily build breastworks made from farmers' fences. One trooper held four horses 200 yards behind the line of battle while three men took direct part in the fighting. Unlike the Confederates, they were armed with breach loading carbines. The breach loaders lacked the range of the rifled muskets but because of their high rate of fire, almost doubled the effective fire power over muzzle loading rifles carried by the Rebel infantry.

Buford's Union cavalry division had 6 light ordinance rifles with wrought iron barrels under the command of Lieutenant John Calef to provide artillery support. Their relatively light weight made them perfect for fast moving cavalry operations. Buford positioned these guns

This image shows the statue of John Buford and the first Union cannon to be fired at the Confederates. The orbs seem to still be protecting the Federal position.

so as to let the Confederates believe the Union position was much larger than his single division. He spread his battery along the McPherson Ridge line by placing two guns north of the Chambersburg Pike, two positioned south of the pike and the remaining two farther to the south near the spot where General Reynolds was soon to be killed. The guns north of the Chambersburg Pike would be the first northern artillery to join the battle as the Rebels approached from the west on the Chambersburg Pike .

The Army of Northern Virginia was short of supplies and was foraging off the land. There were no lines of supply from the South to furnish ammunition or food. A spy working for General Longstreet had brought news that the Army of the Potomac was moving north under their new commander, General Meade. Lee responded to the news by sending couriers to General Ewell with orders to abandon his plan to capture Harrisburg. He was told to return to the Cashtown area and concentrate rebel forces to meet the Army of the Potomac.

On the night of June 30, the Confederate commanders met at the Cashtown Tavern* to discuss their course of action.

General Lee was not present at the meeting, but was with General Longstreet in Chambersburg. The Generals present at Cashtown were well aware of Lee's orders to avoid any engagement with Union

In this image, our friend reads the historical sign outside of the Cashtown Inn along the Chambersburg Pike. On the right side of the picture, you can see an orb with a clearly defined face that appears to be reading over her shoulder. The image of the spirit is partially chopped off by the edge of the frame. I was not aware of the presence of the orb when I snapped the image and almost missed having it in the picture.

troops until all the Southern forces could be concentrated in the area. General J.E.B. Stuart and his cavalry were still on a raid in central Pennsylvania and were currently in Carlisle trying to catch up with Ewell's Corp. General Lee had not heard from him for over a week in spite of his orders to keep in courier contact. Stuart had captured over 100 wagons of Federal supplies and Union prisoners near Rockville, MD that slowed his progress. Additionally, he ran into Union troops in Hanover and was further delayed in his attempt to join General Ewell. As a result of the lack of information, the Rebel commanders at Cashtown were not aware of either Stuart's location or that of the Army of the Potomac.

Without cavalry for reconnaissance, General A.P. Hill and his commanders made the mistaken decision that the Union Column observed by General Pettigrew was indeed local militia. The next day General Heth would take his entire division to Gettysburg and disperse the militia. His division would be followed by that of Maj. General Dorsey Pender. In total, the column would consist of 17,000 infantry and two battalions of artillery. Opposing them would be the 2,700 troopers of Buford's cavalry.

Henry Heth was new to command at the Division level and his inexperience would reflect on the results of the upcoming battle. The Rebels started the Morning of July 1 with no idea they would be engaged in a major battle. General Heth actually had 22 year old Major William Pegram's artillery battalion lead the column toward Gettysburg. Under normal circumstances, the lead units would usually be cavalry but none were available to the confederate commanders. When fired upon by Buford's cavalry, there would be a delay as the infantry units had to move through the artillery caissons to form in a battle formation.

Instead of local militia, the Rebels found the veteran soldiers of Buford's Division intent on defending the town of Gettysburg. They also did not realize that the infantry and artillery of the Union First Corps under General Reynolds was rapidly arriving on the field with the Eleventh Corps close behind. None of the participants were aware that a military engagement of epic proportions was about to take place.

In anticipation of the Rebel advance, General Buford positioned groups of 4 men (videttes) in a line situated along a 4 mile radius from the center of Gettysburg. A total of 275 men were stationed in this line and their job was to signal contact with the advancing enemy. Lt. Marellus Jones of the 8th Illinois Cavalry was in command of the first line of defense and fired the first shot of the battle at a distance of 700 yards to the advancing southerners at about 6:00 am. The shot missed its target but as it was joined by other rounds of musket fire they created confusion among General Heath's Division.

As more shots were fired by the Federal cavalry before retreating to the next line of defense, Heth slowly formed into a line of battle and unlimbered his artillery. Almost two hours were gained by Buford's cavalry until Heth could form his men into battle formation and move forward. Buford's men then fell back to form a line of about 500 men on Herr's Ridge, approximately 1 mile west of the main defensive line on McPherson Ridge. Buford's Cavalry on Herr's Ridge held for almost an hour, gaining the valuable time needed for the soldiers of Reynolds' 1st Corps to begin to arrive and reinforce the McPhearson Ridge defensive line.

As General Heth threw more troops into the fray, the Confederate commanders still did not realize that the entire Army of the Potomac was within a days' march of the town of Gettysburg. General Lee's orders to not engage the enemy was forgotten as the battle moved eastward toward the town of Gettysburg. The timely arrival of General Reynolds' 1st Corp would temporarily change the tide of battle in favor of the Federal troops, but overwhelming Confederate force would carry the day. General Buford summed up the situation perfectly as he stood in the tower of the Lutheran Seminary when General Reynolds arrived and asked him what was happening. His answer was "There'll be hell to pay." Truer words were never spoken.

---

* The Cashtown Tavern was one of the earliest hospital sites of the battle as the first southern casualties were treated in this location. The building is famous for paranormal activities.

Chapter Three

The First Day,
McPherson Farm & Reynolds Woods

A dawn, a Confederate Division consisting of 7,000 veteran fighters commanded by Major General Henry Heth headed for Gettysburg to disperse what was believed to be local militia and get the needed supplies and shoes. (In reality there were no shoe factories in Gettysburg at the time) Heth's division ran into Buford's pickets about 4 miles west of town and the Battle of Gettysburg began. The skirmishing continued for over 3 hours as the Union troops delayed the Rebels and fell back toward the defensive position by General Buford on McPherson Ridge. Buford's men were instructed to dismount, take cover behind fence rows, fight as infantry and hold the line until reinforcements in the form of Reynolds' First Corps arrived. His 2,700 men were armed with breech loading Smith and Sharps carbines that were capable of firing twice as fast as the muzzle loaders of the Rebel Infantry. This additional fire power was instrumental in helping the Union cavalry to delay the southern infantry.

Heth realized that the thin line of Union cavalry on McPherson Ridge was no match for his larger column of men and unlimbered his artillery on Herr's Ridge, approximately 1 mile from the main Union line. It took several hours to organize the troops in an attempt to disperse the Federal cavalry. The Confederate General then ordered his two lead brigades under General James Archer and General Joseph Davis into line of battle and the Confederates began the assault on McPherson Ridge. In spite of the orders not to engage Union troops by General Lee, the Battle of Gettysburg was escalating by the minute.

As General Heth began the assault on McPherson Ridge, General Reynolds arrived with his First Corp at about 10:00 am. He rushed his infantry and artillery in double quick time to the line established by General Buford on McPherson Ridge. The stage was now set for one of the major killing fields of the first day's action with over 2,000 casualties occurring in the area that is now known as Reynolds Woods. General Reynolds, one of the most respected Federal Commanders was immediately killed by a shot to the base of his skull by a southern marksman. The General was attempting to encourage the Michigan regiments of the Iron Brigade to stop the oncoming troops from Alabama, Tennessee, North Carolina and Mississippi. Major General Abner Doubleday then assumed command of the First Corps (no, he did not invent the game of baseball). By night fall of the first day of battle, over 16,000 men were killed, wounded or captured. Death did not discriminate between Generals and privates.

The following picture shows a cloud of ecto mist in the shape of a rearing horse that was taken near the spot where General Reynolds was killed by a Confederate sharpshooter. If you look closely at the picture you can make out the face a soldier clinging to the neck of the horse.

On the morning of July 1, 1863, the Iron Brigade assigned to the First Corp under John Reynolds was rushing in double quick time on the Emmitsburg Pike. Their unit was the first to reinforce Buford's Calvary that was engaged with Henry Heth's Division near the McPherson farm. The story of Michigan's hard fighting Iron Brigade is one of bravery and unsurpassed loyalty to the cause of the Union. Famous for wearing distinctive black "Hardee" hats, the unit came to Gettysburg with nearly 1,900 men fit for combat and left with approximately 750. Battle reports for the Iron Brigade show 1,150 casualties, about 63% that reported for duty would become a casualty of the battle. Opposing Southern units suffered similar casualty statistics.

A regiment of the Iron Brigade, the 24th Michigan was pressed into action in the area of Reynolds Woods so fast that they were not given time to load their muskets. They were ordered to take the field with a fierce bayonet charge. It proved momentarily successful as the Alabama Brigade under the command of General Archer was driven back across Willoughby Run. Almost 200 Confederates were taken prisoner and it appeared the Federals might win the day. Among the Rebels taken prisoner was General Archer himself. The lost time due to the disorganization of the southern forces had given Federal reinforcements time to arrive on the field. For the time being, both sides decided to reorganize and there was a lull in the action as reinforcements continued to arrive for both blue and gray.

The above picture was taken May 14th, 2010 after a series of violent thunder storms left the air hanging heavy with energy. It was taken in Reynolds Woods at the precise spot where the 24th Michigan conducted the successful bayonet charge against the Brigade commanded by General Archer. You can see the monument to the 24th Michigan in the background. A soldier can be seen in the right side of the picture frozen in time in a bayonet charge. Note the soldier is even looking downward to see where he is running and his hands are in the position of holding a musket during a bayonet charge. He is surrounded by a group of orbs. I believe this is a classic example of a residual haunting.

Paranormal activity can take many forms and appearances. An apparition occurs when a figure or shape appears. On occasions the apparitions are part of a cloud, referred to as ectoplasm or ecto mist. These figures are generally not as distinct and often are partial shapes. Sometimes apparitions are solid figures that are impenetrable to light. This type of apparition can be seen in Chapter Ten, "The Peach Orchard."

Concurrent with the charge of the 24th Michigan, Union troops were also counter attacking on the right side of McPherson Ridge, between the Chambersburg Pike and Reynolds Woods. It was in this area that the only civilian known to participate in the battle, 70 year old John Burns, a veteran of the War of 1812, fought side by side with the Iron Brigade and the 150th Pennsylvania Volunteers. He had borrowed a musket from a wounded soldier and requested that the field command-

ers allowed him to help defend his home. He was given permission to fight with the Iron Brigade. A monument memorializing his actions stands near the McPherson barn. The following picture shows his monument with a protecting orb presence.

John Burns fought to protect his home from the southern invaders. Burns was wounded several times during the fight. Burns is the only civilian known to participate in the battle of Gettysburg.

Regimental flags or colors were held in the highest esteem by the fighting men on both sides. The ultimate disgrace was to have the opposing side capture your battle flag. Many units took vows that they would never allow their flags to be captured. On the first day of fighting, the 16th Maine was given the task of holding back the Confederates to cover the retreat of the First Corps.

In the Civil War, the color bearer was a primary target for the opposing side. If the color bearer was hit and the flag dropped, others would rush to carry it. Officers would grab the flag to create a rallying point for the other fighters. Even though it was considered an honor to carry the flag into battle, carrying the colors in the Civil War was the personification of occupational hazards. The 26th North Carolina of Pettigrew's Brigade lost 10 men carrying the flag in the fighting around Reynolds Woods. In the same area, the 24th Michigan of the Iron Brigade lost nine men carrying the colors. In the grand assault of July 3rd, the 11th Mississippi lost 8 color bearers. The courage and bravery of the fighting men on both sides is awe inspiring but that of the color bearers is almost beyond belief.

The next photograph is a figure in a cloud of ectoplasm that was taken in the area of the charge of the 7th Michigan. It shows a Union color bearer carrying the Federal colors. If you look closely you can see the stripes of the flag.

It is almost impossible to grasp the carnage of the initial fighting. Southern General Henry Heth entered the fighting with about 7,000 men and in 25 minutes lost about 2,700 seasoned veterans. His main opponents, the Iron Brigade lost almost ¾ of the unit's men. General Heth was wounded when a bullet grazed the side of his head. His life was saved because his hat was too big and he had put newspaper inside the band to make it fit. The newspaper deflected the bullet saving his life, but knocking him senseless.

With Generals Heth injured, Archer captured, and A.P. Hill not present on the field of battle, confusion created a lull in the fighting as Rebel troops were reorganized. During this lull, both sides were rushing reinforcements to the scene of the fighting. General Ewell's Corp would soon arrive from the north and the commitment of his forces would assure that a major battle would be fought around the town of Gettysburg. When Lee finally arrived on the field in the early afternoon, he found Federal forces in full retreat through the streets of Gettysburg. By the time of his arrival, his forces were firmly committed to the battle. As Lee surveyed the early accomplishments of his generals, he issued orders for the total commitment of his troops, confident that the Army of the Potomac faced total destruction.

In the picture above, a soldier peers from the brush in the area held by General Archer's North Carolina brigade. This section of Reynolds Woods was the site of the some of the most intense fighting on the first day and is the area of very active paranormal activity.

A light emitting orb is photographed by the monument to the 142nd Pennsylvania Regiment. This monument stands along the McPherson Ridge defensive line held by the General Buford's cavalry and reinforced by the Union 1st Corps. The regiment suffered heavy losses when overwhelmed by the advancing rebels.

Pictured below is a detail of the Elliot map for the first day fighting in the area of McPherson Ridge showing Confederate and Union mass grave sites. The spot where General Reynolds was shot is clearly marked. Grave sites of southerners buried by their own troops were not marked on the map. Since the Rebels held this area through the 4th of July it is safe to assume many of the fallen were buried in un-marked graves and were never re-interred.

As shown on the Elliott map, in 1863 there was a toll house on the Chambersburg Pike near Willoughby Run. The wooded area to the south, where the fighting oc-curred, was clear of under-brush and the trees provided cover for both sides. Many of the Rebel

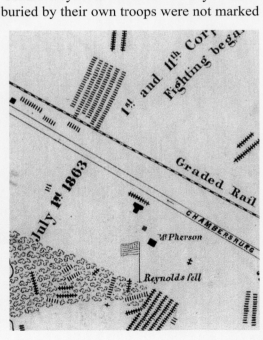

dead were buried on the north side of the Chambersburg Pike while the bulk of the Federal troops were buried near the spot where General Reynolds was killed.

Orbs north of Chambersburg Pike at the site of Confederate graves.

The next photograph shows another image peering from the woods in the area of the charge by the 24th Michigan toward the position of Archer's Brigade. This is an area of heavy paranormal activities because of the intense action that took place on the first day of fighting. Entire units lost their ability to function as a result of the heavy fighting at what is now known as Reynolds Woods.

Spirits are present throughout the battle field in many forms and shapes. You usually find them peering from behind bushes and trees much like they did as soldiers in life. There is residual haunting where you see an object such as a cannon or an intelligent haunting where there is interaction with the spirit. Throughout this book I will relate instances where the haunting is incredibly intelligent to the point of physical interaction.

While there were many heroes in the fighting of the first day, the decisions and execution of General Buford's plan of battle saved the day for the Union. He was the first to realize the tactical advantage of fighting from the high ground in the Gettysburg area. His defense in depth plan bought enough time for the First Corps to arrive and reinforce the initial lines of battle. The delay caused by Buford's cavalry, outnumbered almost 8 to 1, allowed enough troops from the Eleventh Corps to arrive and hold the fall back position on Cemetery Hill. If the Confederates had been allowed to carry the field earlier in the day, they could have overwhelmed Cemetery Hill and the outcome of the battle, and maybe even the war, would have been far different.

The area of Reynolds Woods has produced some of the most spectacular paranormal pictures featured in this edition. Both sides fought with an incredible intensity and violence that is still being carried out by their spirits almost 150 years later on this hallowed ground.

The form on the left shows the plasma cloud shape of another charging soldier in the area of the 24th Michigan. While most of his body is obscured, his face is clearly seen. This image was enhanced to bring out the detail of the soldier. The surrounding orbs also have strong facial images.

Chapter Four

The Railroad Cut

As the fighting of July 1st developed on nearby McPherson Ridge, an unfinished railroad belonging to the Gettysburg and Hanover Railroad would become critical to the outcome of the fighting. The railroad cut had been excavated in anticipation of extending the rail line to Chambersburg from Gettysburg but the track had not as yet been laid. In the initial phase of the fighting, General Buford had positioned two of his guns between the Chambersburg Pike and the Railroad cut.

Immediately upon arriving on the scene, the First Corps unlimbered it's artillery on McPherson Ridge and began a devastating fire on the approaching Confederate columns on the Chambersburg Pike. As a Confederate Brigade under General Joseph R. Davis moved to the North of the Chambersburg Pike in an attempt to flank the Federal troops, they came under heavy fire from the reserve Regiment of the Iron Brigade, the 6th Wisconsin. Two Union regiments from Cutlers Brigade joined in the attack on Davis's troops. With heavy musket fire on their flank and front, the Rebel troops made a fatal mistake. They took cover in the unfinished railroad cut and began to fire upon the flank of the Union troops. The 2nd and 42nd Mississippi regiments were about to find out that the apparent safety of the railroad cut was actually a trap, the sides of the cut were too steep to climb, especially under direct fire from the attacking Federal troops.

The heavy Southern return fire from the railroad cut endangered the Federal line held by the 1st Corp east of what is now Reynolds Woods. Lieutenant Colonel Rufus Dawes of the 6th Wisconsin realized that the Confederates had to be dislodged from the railroad cut if they were to hold the McPherson Ridge defensive line.

Dawes led his 6th Wisconsin Regiment in a heroic, bloody charge across open ground between the Chambersburg Pike and the railroad cut. He was supported by the 84th New York regiment, one of the few units to see action all three days of the battle.

This monument to the 84th New York stands in tribute to one of the few regiments that actually fought on all 3 days of the battle. Shown with the monument by the railroad is an unusual light emitting orb. They assisted the 6th Wisconsin in the charge that killed and captured a large number of the members of the Mississippi infantry in the unfinished railroad cut.

The charge trapped the Confederates firing from the railroad cut because they could not retreat by climbing the steep side hill. As a result of the southern troops being trapped like fish in a barrel, many were killed and over 200 made the prudent decision to surrender. Colonel Dawes lost almost 60% of the Federal soldiers involved in the charge. The arrival of the First Corps temporarily saved the day for the North. Heth pulled back his troops to reorganize and await the arrival of the Southern reinforcements that were streaming toward Gettysburg.

Not only were southern troops arriving from the West but Ewell's Corps was arriving from the town of Carlisle, situated north of Gettysburg. Early's Division of Ewell's Corp arrived and set up their artillery on the high ground of Oak Hill from which they could fire upon the entire Union defensive line with their rifled guns. Federal troops took sanctuary in the unfinished railroad cut that had just proven disastrous to the rebels earlier in the day as the southern fire coming from the high ground to the North intensified.

General Heth continued to throw more Rebel troops into the fight for McPherson Ridge. In order to dislodge the Federal troops from the rail road cut, two cannon were placed to fire up the bottom of the cut to the west of the Union position. This artillery fire drove the 149th Pennsylvania in a hasty retreat toward the town of Gettysburg. By mid day the overwhelming number of southern troops broke the McPherson Ridge defensive line and forced the Union retreat back through the complicated streets of Gettysburg.

A bright neon orb overlooks the rail road cut that was the scene of violent fighting on the first day.   Note the facial features in the orb.

As the retreat turned into a rout, Federal forces once again used the railroad cut for cover as they ran toward Gettysburg in an attempt to reach the relative safety of the fortifications on Cemetery Hill while being hotly pursued by Southern troops. The railroad cut now became a killing field for Federal soldiers as it had been earlier in the day for the Rebels. This heavy loss of life makes the Rail Road cut and the adjoining fields a source of active paranormal activity.

Looking southeast adjacent to the Rail Road you find the 95th New York and the 6th Wisconsin regimental statues pictured on the next page. A huge orb guards 95th New York monument while the blue orb on the left has a distinct face.

The 6th Wisconsin is the acknowledged hero of the battle for the Rail Road cut. It charged the Southern troops that were directing musket fire from the protection of the rail road cut. When they charged across the open field they sustained a casualty rate in excess of 60%.

Paranormal photography often results in images of the unknown. After the thousands of photographs taken on the battle field, I had thought I had seen it all. When I took the picture shown at the bottom of the next page, I had no idea what the object in the lower left corner represented. It was fairly large and did not resemble anything I had seen

before. Puzzled by the image, I emailed the picture to Steve McNaughton, author of several books on the paranormal who is quite knowledgeable in the unknown and an individual that I trust for an honest opinion. The reply from Steve was definitely not what I expected. Without my knowledge, two weeks earlier he had interviewed a 7 year old clairvoyant who disclosed as part of the interview that she played with fairies. Steve asked her to draw the image of a fairy so he would recognize it if he ever saw one. His response to my email was that the image in the photograph matched her drawing done two weeks earlier. That image is shown below in the photo recorded in the railroad cut.

At the time I recorded the image on the previous page, I had probably reviewed over 30,000 pictures of the battlefield and never saw anything like the shape in the left foreground of the picture. About two months later I photographed a similar picture near the Eternal Flame that appears in Chapter Five. Clairvoyants refer to the presence of elementals, fairies and angels but this is the first time I had ever personally experienced such an image. I showed the picture to another friend of mine that is sensitive to the spirit world without any comment on my part. Her answer was "Oh my God, it's a fairy."

Most visitors drive across the bridge over the rail road cut without realizing the importance to the battle and the loss of life in the area. Most of the visitors also fail to realize the frequency of paranormal activities in the area.

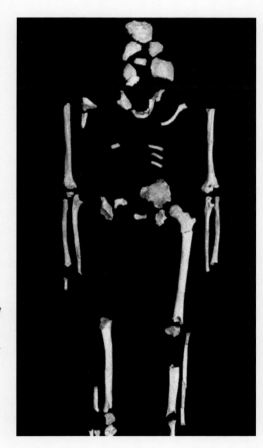

Bones of a soldier buried next to the railroad cut. These remains were recovered in the mid-1990s.

Chapter Five

Oak Hill & Iverson's Pits

As the battle progressed on July 1st, a small hill with a large apple orchard became very important to the Confederates. The hill gave the Rebels control of the area by using it as an artillery platform. Rifled cannon of the time had an effective range of 2,000 yards, more than adequate to fire upon the entire Federal McPhearson Ridge defensive line from this position. Known as Oak Hill and currently the site of the Eternal Light, this area of high ground became an ideal spot for artillery to fire upon Union positions near the McPherson Farm and around Barlow Knoll. As the day progressed on July 1, Barlow Knoll, Oak Ridge and McPherson Ridge rapidly became the Federal primary line of defense. Shortly after noon the infantry division of Rebel General Robert E. Rodes arrived and formed on the North side of Oak Hill, unseen by Union forces. Artillery batteries were placed in the vicinity of what is now the area of the Eternal Light and very effective flanking fire commenced on the Union Line.

From the north side of Oak Hill, cannon could fire on what is now known as Barlow Knoll, the right flank of the Union line. The Eleventh Corps was assigned to this position in what would prove to be the impossible task of holding the right flank of the Union line west of town. Union gunners returned fire on the Rebel batteries with some success, but could not stop the Confederate barrage from the higher ground. Union troops took cover from the artillery in the railroad cut that had proven so disastrous for southern troops earlier in the day. As more and more rebel troops poured into the area, the Federal soldiers would be overwhelmed, creating the massive retreat through Gettysburg.

One unit that was overwhelmed in this area was the 16th Maine. Ordered to hold their position at any costs along what is now Doubleday Avenue, after 3 hours of intense fighting it became apparent that they would be overrun and captured. The survivors tore their regimental

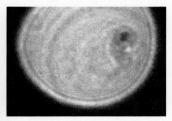

This huge orb at Oak Hill shows the facial shape of a nose with what I believe is a bullet hole in the area of the eye. There is also coloration around the bullet hole that could be attributed to blood from the wound.

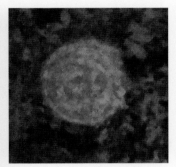

This spirit orb was also photographed in the vicinity of the Eternal Light on Oak Hill. Note the well defined eyes that seem to be watching the old field of battle.

flag into small pieces and the solders hid the strips on their person so the Rebels would not take their flag. There is probably no greater example of the high esteem that soldiers of either side had for their regimental colors.

President Franklin Roosevelt dedicated the Eternal flame monument in 1933 to celebrate the 75th anniversary of the battle. My personal belief is the flame helps generate energy that makes this Oak Hill an area of significant paranormal activity.

The photograph below was taken near the current location of the Eternal Flame monument. This is the same shaped image that was discussed in the Chapter Four, "The Railroad Cut." If you didn't believe it was a fairy in Chapter Three, you probably won't believe it here either.

In what turned out to be one of the most misdirected decisions of the battle, General Rhodes ordered General Alfred Iverson's Brigade of troops from North Carolina to form into line of battle and attack the Union flank on Oak Ridge, near what is now the site of the low observation tower on Doubleday Avenue. Iverson began the advance with no attempt at reconnaissance or advancing skirmishers to define the position of Union troops (skirmishers in the civil war were the equivalent of a canary in a coal mine, the first to die). Unknown to the advancing North Carolinians, the Union regiments of Brig. General Baxter's Brigade were hiding undetected behind a stone wall directly in their path. Baxter allowed the Rebels to get within 100 yards of his hidden position, rose and fired a barrage of musket fire into Iverson's Brigade killing as many as 200 men in a single volley. With no cover available, the rest of the brigade fell to the ground and continued to suffer casualties. A small monument exists today in the spot where many of Iverson's men and flags were captured. The portion of Elliott's map shows the area of the mass burial site of Iverson's men.

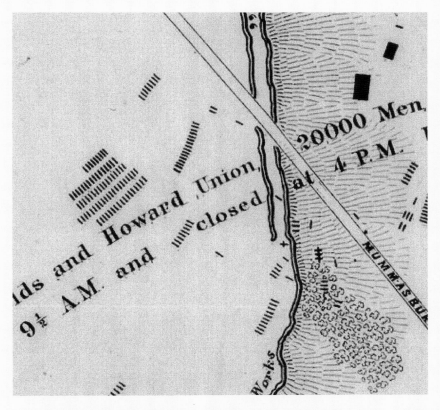

Witnesses described the dead bodies of the North Carolina soldiers being lined up in almost a straight line where they fell. The remains of Iverson's men were reburied in the South in the years after the war, but depressions were left in the ground that became known as Iverson's Pits. Farmers at the time told stories of how the crops grew much higher in the area of the depressions in the ground. The depressions are long gone but the spirits of the men who died that day remain. The local farmers also told stories of how human bones would be plowed to the surface for years after the rebel bodies were removed to be reburied in the south. Some historians believe that many bodies could remain in the area. Perhaps these remaining bodies are the reason paranormal activity is quite common in the area of Iverson's Pits and Oak Ridge. An example of such activity is the photo below where a soldier looks at the camera from the exact location of the pits. If you look closely at the photo you can even see the mustache of the soldier. This is truly an area of great paranormal activity.

Paranormal activity can repeat itself in the same location over extended time frames. There is a grove of trees located across Doubleday Avenue from Iverson's Pits. Whenever I am in the area I make a point of taking multiple pictures. Last fall when the leaves were off the trees,

I took a picture that had a full bodied apparition of a Confederate Calvary officer. The southern soldier was standing at the back edge of the woods looking through the trees at the camera. When I enlarged the picture, the image of the high riding boots and short officer's jacket of the Confederate cavalry became apparent. The image of the Confederate officer is shown on the previous page along with an enlargement to show the detail of the soldier. Also note the location of the apparition with respect to the trees.

About 9 months later I was in the same location and took the picture of the full bodied apparition shown below. Note that it is the same spirit in the same location. The only difference is there are leaves on the trees. Interestingly, the Elliott map shows a couple of Confederate graves in that area.

This the only time I have photographed exactly the same spirit in exactly the same place. Whenever you go back to the spot there is generally activity in the form of orbs but the appearance of the apparition is a rare event.

My curiosity was aroused over why an apparition would appear at exactly the same place over an extended period of time. One late sum-

mer evening, I asked a medium that works with our group to accompany myself and several investigators to go to the spot and try to make contact with the Confederate soldier. I had seen her provide names of spirits in the past where research proved her to be correct. The proximity to Iverson's Pits had a very negative effect on her and she was actually overcome with physical pain similar to the suffering of the soldiers, but not before she contacted what she said was a Rebel lieutenant. She said that the last name of the Confederate soldier was Reed and she believed that his first name was Steven and he was a lieutenant of cavalry. Before we could extract any more information, we had to take her from the site because of her physical discomfort.

I tried to research the name "Reed" in many of the usual sources with no success. The "Gettysburg Death Roster" by Robert Krick and Chris Ferguson is the most definitive list of Confederate dead at the battle of Gettysburg. Considered 85% accurate because of poor Rebel records, the book is a very reliable reference guide. While there were several Reeds listed, none of the units fought on Oak Ridge.

Modern technology on the internet allows us to research names in ways never before possible. I discovered a site that lists names and information from tomb stones; unfortunately I had to subscribe to try it. General Rodes' division had fought in the area with troops mostly from North Carolina but a search of that state came back empty. By this stage of the conflict, regiments had been reorganized and soldiers from other states such as South Carolina may have been intermingled with the Tar Heels. When I searched the state of South Carolina I found the following information recorded on a tombstone in Abbeville, South Carolina. A soldier with the name Reed, **born 12-11-1837 fell in front of Battle of Gettysburg 7-2-63.** While there may have been more than one Rebel soldier named Reed killed in the Battle of Gettysburg, I firmly believe that the clairvoyant once again identified the correct name of a spirit that still makes its presence known to persons willing to understand the paranormal world. What makes this story even more interesting is that this soldiers name is not included in the list of Confederate Dead at Gettysburg.

In the same area along Doubleday Avenue you will find the monument to the 11th Pennsylvania Regiment. This monument is one of only two monuments on the battlefield that include a dog. The other monument with a dog is the Irish Brigade's Celtic Cross located at the edge of the Wheatfield. Sallie was the mascot of the 11th Pennsylvania and was present during the intense fighting that forced the unit to retreat to the fortified protection of Cemetery Hill. When the soldiers regrouped they realized that Sallie was missing and presumed she had been killed. On July 4, the unit returned to Oak Ridge to bury their dead and found Sallie guarding the dead soldiers from her Regiment. She was emaciated from having no food or water for three days while under the hot sun, but the soldiers nursed her back to health. She continued to provide inspiration to her unit until the final months of the war.

Just two months before the end of the conflict, the 11th Pennsylvania was at Hatchers Run, Virginia. The night before the battle, Sallie kept crawling into the tent of her care givers, crying and keeping them awake. It was the first time she had ever behaved like that and the men kept putting her out of the tent to get some sleep. The next day Sallie and the three soldiers were all killed in action.

In the world of the paranormal, a lot is unexplained.

A bright orb near the monument to the 11th Pennsylvania Infantry. The likeness of Sallie is on the far side of the monument.

Chapter Six

The Union Right Flank, Barlow Knoll

As the fighting progressed on the first day, the Eleventh Corps secured the Union right flank on a piece of elevated ground that was known at the time as Blotcher's Knoll. This corps consisted largely of men of German decent. Many of the soldiers could not speak English and were commanded by German officers. As a twist of fate, the Eleventh Corps had been humiliated two months earlier at Chancellorsville. Confederates under Stonewall Jackson attacked the unprotected Union right flank and forced the Eleventh Corps into a panicked rout. Bearing the brunt of the rebel attack at Chancellorsville was the German speaking 153rd Pennsylvania Infantry. On this day they again were put into a position where bravery and hard fighting would not be enough to hold their precarious position. After the Battle of Gettysburg their Corps would be referred to as "the Flying Dutchmen;" definitely not a compliment.

General Francis Barlow had been given the command of the 1st Division of the Eleventh Corps after their humiliation at Chancellorsville in an effort to restore their morale. A strict disciplinarian, his efforts created additional animosity, especially by the German troops. Barlow had studied law and graduated first in his class at Harvard. Slight of build and 27 years of age when war broke out in 1861 he enlisted as a private in the 12th New York Militia. By June 1863 he had been promoted through the ranks to Brig. General. Until this time he performed admirably. His decisions made on this day would place the soldiers of the whole corps in an untenable position and contribute to the rout of Northern troops through the streets of Gettysburg.

As soon as the Eleventh Corps took their position on the knoll, Confederate artillery began to target them from atop Oak Hill and from up the Harrisburg Road. The batteries sent shot and shell into the thin line of the Union regiments along the length of the Federal defensive position. Three Union batteries responded and the battle for the Northern right flank was in high gear. The battle was joined by a brigade from Rodes' Division. At this time Southern reinforcements in the form of the 8,500-man Confederate Second Corps under the command of General Richard Ewell arrived from the northeast. In the days before the battle, troops from Ewell's Corps had advanced as far as Harrisburg and York, terrorizing the local residents and gathering supplies. One curious fact of the battle of Gettysburg is the Southern troops advanced from the north and Northern troops advanced from the south.

Upon their arrival on the field, Ewell's 1st Division under Jubal Early formed into line of battle and joined in the assault. Ewell was under orders to march to Cashtown and unite with Lee, but took it upon himself to head toward the sound of gun fire. His decision would play a huge role in the first day's success for the Confederates. When Ewell committed his forces to the battle, it was the true point of no return. What could have been a reconnaissance in force would now turn into a major engagement.

With the arrival of the Confederate Second Corps, the Federal Eleventh Corps was now being attacked on two sides as well as the recipient of heavy artillery fire from Oak Hill. The overwhelming Confederate force broke the Union lines around the Alms House and the Union retreat through the town of Gettysburg, to the safety of Cemetery Hill had begun. The retreat turned into a rout as panicked Federals found Rebel troops on their heels in hot pursuit. However, the Confederate units became disorganized as they chased the retreating Federals through the complicated streets of Gettysburg. So many Union prisoners were taken that it only added to the confusion and slowed the Rebel pursuit. The confusion continued, and with the disorganization of the Rebel units, General Early could not regroup in time to assault Cemetery Hill before night fall of the first day.

The pictures on the following pages show that paranormal activity often repeats itself as spirits tend to remain at the same location.

General Barlow was seriously wounded three times in the fighting and left for dead on the field of battle by his men. According to the memoirs of General John Gordon, the Rebel commander in the area known to embellish the facts a bit in later life, he found the injured Barlow and sent him to a field hospital thereby saving his life. Contrary to this account, Barlow never mentioned Gordon saving his life in any of his post war writings. When the Rebels retreated on July 4th, they left the badly wounded Barlow behind and he was recovered by Union

These pictures showing a huge orb were taken almost a year apart. Note the similarity in the unusual size and color of the orb in both images.

troops. Barlow's wife was a nurse with the Sanitary Commission and nursed him back to health. It was almost a year until he would recover from his wound and return to duty. The elevated ground where he fought is now known as Barlow Knoll in his honor. The Eleventh Corps actually fought bravely against overwhelming odds. Their leaders put them in untenable positions and repeatedly made mistakes that caused their defeats at Chancellorsville and Gettysburg. In some instances the officers could not speak German and looked down on the immigrants that joined together to defend the Union even though they could not speak the language of the Republic.

Brigadier General Alexander Schimmelfennig's Brigade was positioned next to Barlow's Division near the knoll. As his men retreated through the town of Gettysburg, he managed to save himself from capture by hiding in a pigsty behind a house on Baltimore Street. He hid there for three days while the town was occupied by Confederates. The legend of the "Flying Dutchmen" was certainly further enhanced by the plight of the pigsty General.

The old Gettysburg Alms House is gone but Barlow Knoll and the old Alms House Cemetery is part of the Auto Tour and a great place for paranormal abnormalities.

When the remnants of the Eleventh Corps arrived at Cemetery Hill, it was reorganized and placed in the first line of defense at the eastern

In an image taken at the extreme right flank of the Union line, a spirit looks toward what would have been the old Alms House. This is where the Eleventh Corps bore the brunt of the overwhelming strength of the Confederate attack. In spite of fighting bravely, they did not have the manpower or artillery support to defend against the numerically superior Southern troops.

The Eleventh Corps was placed on Barlow Knoll to defend the right flank of the Union Line on the first day. A spirit figure looks toward the area of heavy casualties and the location of the old Gettysburg Alms House. The Alms House cemetery is about 100 yards from this location.

base of the hill. The next evening these men would bear the full brunt of the Confederate assault on East Cemetery Hill. They would once again be overwhelmed by numerical superiority on the part of the Rebel attackers.

The Alms House cemetery behind Barlow Knoll provided burial for the indigent of Adams County. This grave yard was the scene of hard fighting as the Eleventh Corps was driven from the area. Several soldiers were buried in the cemetery after the battle. Here a bright red orb is seen over the Alms House grave stones.

*The orb moves rapidly by the monument at Barlow Knoll.
A pair of eyes seem to be looking at the camera.*

Chapter Seven

East Cemetery Hill

IRONICALLY, Eleventh Corps commander General Oliver Howard was the first to realize the importance of using Cemetery Hill as a defensive fall back position. His placement of his Second Division under General Adolf von Steinwehr provided the rallying position during the rout of the first day. Without the fortification of Cemetery Hill, the outcome of the entire battle would have been far different.

General Lee rode into Gettysburg on the afternoon of July 1 and sent orders to General Ewell to follow up with an attack on the newly reinforced Union positions on Cemetery Hill. Lee knew that time would work to his disadvantage as large numbers of the Army of the Potomac were in close proximity of Gettysburg and marching to the sound of gunfire. General Ewell proved unable to execute the desired attack on the Union positions. His men were exhausted from the days fighting and disorganized because of the pursuit of the Union troops. In addition, they had a large number of Union prisoners to deal with.

In the late afternoon on July 1, the Union troops were being driven through Gettysburg to the high ground of East Cemetery Hill. Originally known as "Raffensberger's Hill" for the local land owner, it would become known as Cemetery Hill after the Evergreen Cemetery that was on its summit. General Winfield Scott Hancock, commander of the Second Corps, arrived on the scene about 4:30 in the afternoon of the first day with orders from General Meade to take temporary command of the army. Upon his arrival, he was faced with the chaos of Federal troops in full retreat from their defeat at the McPhearson farm and the entire right flank of the Union Line.

Hancock immediately tried to maintain some semblance of order and reinforce the Union positions on the high ground. By the morning of July 2, artillery was in lunettes (earthen barricades), infantry was behind fortifications and this high ground was now the most heavily fortified area of the battlefield. The Eleventh Corps, following their defeat at Barlow Knoll, was rallied and placed at the base of Cemetery Hill as the first line of defense against the anticipated Rebel attack. When the attack came on the evening of July 2, they would once again fail to hold the line against the overwhelming Confederate force.

The first day of the battle ended with almost 15,000 casualties, 9,000 for the North and 6,000 for the South. Federal troops were forced to retreat in a rout and it looked to General Lee that a southern victory was assured. However, as night fell, the Union forces were in a fortified defensive position on Cemetery Hill and many Federal reinforcements were arriving hourly. By driving the retreating Federal troops to the high ground, the Confederates had actually done the Union a favor by forcing them to consolidate men and equipment on Cemetery Hill. General Lee's troops now had to take the offensive and attack strong Union

As evening of July 2 fell, the Rebels charged East Cemetery Hill in the failing light. Union positions overrun in this area with a high casualty count. Once again the Flying Dutchmen lived up to their reputation. A soldier still looks for the action from the location of the defensive line at the base of Cemetery Hill.

positions on the high ground to win the battle, a situation that would contribute to the defeat of General Lee's war machine, the Army of Northern Virginia.

General Lee's plan for the second day was to have Longstreet attack the Union left flank in the vicinity of Little Round Top while General Ewell attacked the right flank on Culp's and Cemetery Hills. The coordinated attack would prevent General Meade from moving reinforcements freely. Unfortunately for the South, by the afternoon of the second day Lee's plans were not going well. Longstreet was delayed in getting his corps in position to attack the Federal left flank until almost 4:00 pm. At the sound of Longstreet's guns, Ewell chose to begin his attack with an artillery barrage from Benner Hill, almost 1 mile away from Culp's and Cemetery Hill instead of initiating an infantry assault. Southern batteries on Benner Hill were situated 50 feet lower in eleva-

The presence of the spirits of animals is a reoccurring event on the battlefield. Near the summit of East Cemetery Hill there are lunettes that were thrown up to protect the cannon crews from musket fire. This image of a ghost dog was taken at one of the earthen breastworks where artillery was captured by the Rebel troops on the evening of the first day. Several months later I took the picture of this same ghost dog on East Cavalry Field. Having a pet ghost dog is really weird.

tion than their Federal opponents, a huge disadvantage for the cannons of the time. Union batteries from Cemetery Hill responded and their counter battery fire drove the Southern cannon from Benner Hill while killing the best Rebel artillerist, 19 year old "Boy Major" Joseph W. Latimer. Lee's plan of battle had General Early attack the northeast side of Cemetery Hill while General Rodes would attack the northwest side of the fortified Federal position. Delays would prevent Rodes from carrying out his part of the coordinated attack.

It was not until dusk fell on the evening of the second day that Rebel troops under the command of General Harry Hays and Colonel Isaac Avery began the attack on East Cemetery Hill. About this time the fighting by the First Corps on the left flank of the line had subsided. Led by the famous "Louisiana Tigers," the Confederates broke the Eleventh Corps line and actually captured a Union battery on the crest of the hill, fighting in the dark. Rodes had finally gotten into position but realized the futility of attacking fortified positions in the dark. His failure to attack as Lee had planned meant that no one would support the Southern advance on the crest of Cemetery Hill.

This image was taken at the place where the Louisiana Tigers advanced to temporally capture Federal guns.

With no additional support for the Southerners on the hill, a counter attack by the Union Second Corps cleared the summit and secured East Cemetery Hill for the duration of the battle. Colonel Avery, one of the South's most able commanders would fall mortally wounded during the assault on the hill. Only conjecture will answer the question of what would have happened if Rodes had been able to coordinate his attack on Cemetery Hill.

The Eleventh Corps, placed at the base of Cemetery Hill was the first line of defense for the Union troops in the area. Exhausted and emotionally drained from being driven from the defensive line of Barlow

As General Avery led his attack against Cemetery Hill, there was a large loss of life near the bottom of the hill. This spirit peers from the trees, probably still looking for the Rebel reinforcements that never came.

The exhausted and demoralized Eleventh Corps was placed along the base of Cemetery Hill to act as the first line of defense. In the image above you can see orbs throughout the entire area but on the right edge of the picture, a soldier peers from the grass toward what would have been the attacking Rebels.

This unusual image was taken at the point of the maximum advance of the Louisiana Tigers. The next frame was clear of any activity.

Knoll on the first day, the "Flying Dutchmen" were not able to hold the line when the Rebels attacked on the evening of July 2. When the Eleventh Corps entered the battle on July 1, it boasted a fighting force of 8,500 men. After being placed in some of the most difficult deployments against overwhelming Confederate forces it suffered a casualty rate of 44%, mostly in its 1st Division and 3rd Divisions.

East Cemetery Hill is one of the most accessible areas of the battlefield. Situated within easy walking distance of historic Gettysburg, hundreds of thousands of visitors tour this area of the battlefield each year. Few realize that the defense of these few acres of land had a huge impact on the outcome of the war. Many brave men on both sides fought to their last breath to control the area known as East Cemetery Hill.

The Evergreen Cemetery dates to 1854 and sat on the high ground that would become a Federal strong point. This image shows the gate house with orbs, especially in the entrance arch. A close-up shows a ghostly image looking out of the window.

Chapter Eight

Day Two, The Rose Farm

As the sun rose on July 2, farmer John Rose had no idea of the carnage that was about to take place on his 236 acre property. Situated along the Emmittsburg Road, his woods, peach orchard and wheat field became names known forever in military history. The house and barn would become a military hospital and a thousand bodies were buried in close proximity. According to accounts, one of the Rose daughters went insane as the bodies were being exhumed in the years after the battle. The Rose family fled before the battle began and the property was not occupied at the time of the battle. The barn served as a Confederate field hospital during the fighting. As the Rebels retreated from the area, they left the most seriously injured to be cared for by Federal doctors. When the Roses returned after the battle, they found the house and barn literally destroyed by the troops. With his crops and livestock gone, John Rose faced financial ruin. Although the house itself is privately owned, the portions of the property, especially the wooded areas that are part of the park are highly spiritual and active with paranormal activity.

On the morning of the second day, Major General Dan Sickles made a decision to re-position his Third Corps in direct contradiction to General Meade's orders. This decision affected the entire outcome of what became the bloodiest day of the battle. Unhappy with the position assigned to him in the middle of the Cemetery Ridge defensive line, he re-positioned his troops in a salient that reached from the peach orchard of farmer Rose, through the wheat field to a bizarre outcropping of rocks that is now known as Devils Den. His position would feel the full strength of the Rebel attack and put General Meade's entire battle plan at risk.

General Joseph Kershaw's Brigade of South Carolina troops was assigned the task of dislodging the Union Third Corps from the peach orchard. His Brigade was assigned ten 12 pound Napoleons which he placed on the south side of the Emmittsburg Road. These guns opened the fighting with concentrated fire on the Federal guns along Wheatfield Road. Awaiting the Confederates were 6 batteries consisting of 30 cannon aligned along Wheatfield Road. Lying in wait in front of the guns were the 3rd Maine and 3rd Michigan regiments of the Union Third Corps, once again holding the high ground.

Kershaw's Brigade passed by the Rose farm house and barn in lines of battle. As they approached the peach orchard the Federal artillery fire was joined by musket ball. The Rose house was located approximately 500 yards from the peach orchard, well within the range of accurate fire. The Rebel advance was met with murderous fire as shot and canister from the artillery placed along the peach orchard ridge line struck the advancing Rebels. When the fighting of the day ended, Kershaw reported the loss of over 600 men from his brigade alone, over half of the men fit to fight on that day. His second regiment went into battle with 40 men and had 4 remain unhurt. Rebel dead were buried in mass shallow graves in the vicinity of where they fell. The Rose house and barn became a military hospital and bodies of the dead were buried around the buildings.

The original Rose Farm barn burned many years ago but the remains of the foundation can still be seen. This picture taken near the barn foundation shows one of the largest concentrations of orbs I have ever observed in one location.

If you look closely, you can see some of the faces of the soldiers and part of the remaining barn wall. A few frames later the area was clear of orbs.

A soldier peers from the grass along the entrance to the Rose Farm. Rebel troops were under heavy artillery fire from the cannon of the Union Third Corps as they crossed the lane of the Rose Farm in this area.

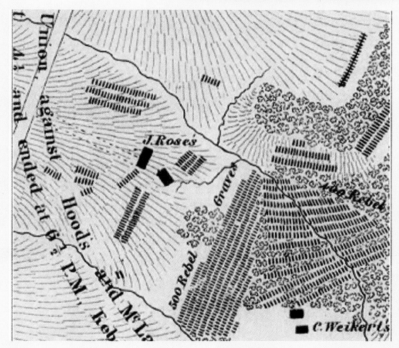

It is often hard to visualize the scope of the carnage that occurred in Gettysburg. This section of the Elliot map shows the mass graves in the vicinity of the Rose farm and Rose woods. Keep in mind that this map only shows Southern grave sites dug by Union troops, not the grave sites where the Confederates buried their own dead.

A walking path runs from the base of Triangle Field through Rose's Woods, crosses Rose's Run and continues to the Wheatfield near the Stoney Ridge. This path runs directly through the area of Rose's Woods where Confederate dead were buried in hand dug trenches. I can think of no other area that had a higher concentration of graves. On a dark night it is one of the more creepy areas of the battlefield with open spaces in the trees and places where vegetation refuses to grow. The canopy of trees blocks the sky so moon and star light can't reach the ground, creating an intense darkness that seems to exemplify the carnage and death that took place here. The picture below was taken on the walking path in the center of Rose's Woods.

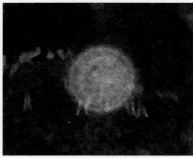

Taken in Rose's Woods at the spot of the mass graves, this orb from the center of the picture has the face of a dog. This is the third picture in this volume that shows the image of an animal.

The existance of animal spirits is not uncommon in the world of paranormal investigations. Their presence can be seen in spirit orbs or full body apparitions as shown in Chapter Seven where a ghost dog is looking over an artillery lunette. We have seen times during paranormal investigations where animal behavior will indicate a spiritual presence. Apparently their senses are more attuned to the spirit world than those of humans.

A field of orbs appears at the edge of Rose's woods. The close up on the right shows a figure peering through the grass on the right side of the picture.

When dealing with the paranormal, I often work with a very reputable medium that lives in our area. I have been with her on various investigations and I am astonished by the information that she supplies without prior knowledge of the happenings in the area being investigated. I have seen her supply the names of spirits that additional research reveals are buried in nearby cemeteries. She has described the physical appearance of deceased individuals accurately without any prior knowledge of the person. One night in September I took her to the Rose farm because I had been photographing the same spirit on numerous occasions and wanted to try to understand why there was so much activity in the area.

Upon arriving at the stone wall at the edge of the Rose Woods where so many of the Confederates were buried in mass graves, she made contact with a Rebel soldier. When she asked his name, the Rebel spirit replied, "Procter, ma'am." He then proceeded to tell her the story of a girl that that would put flowers on the grave sites after the battle and actually care for the graves. The soldier referred to her as "Little Rose." All of a sudden I realized that without any prior knowledge of John Rose's family, she was telling the story of the daughter that eventually went insane as the confederate graves were being opened up so the bodies could be taken back to the south for permanent burial.

While many of the landowners in the Gettysburg area were affected by the battle, none were more devastated than John Rose. He owned the wheatfield, peach orchard, Rose's woods and the stoney hill, scene of the harshest fighting on the second day. With thousands of men killed on his property, it is little wonder that his land remains a source of major paranormal activity.

In this picture the medium is standing by the wall at Rose's woods which was the site of southern mass graves. She is relating the story of Farmer Rose's daughter caring for the Confederate grave sites after the battle as told to her by a Confederate spirit. Note the spirit orb that is directly in front of her face as she relates the story. In telling us the story she became so overcome by emotion that she broke down in tears. The Confederate soldier referred to the young girl as "Little Rose."

Chapter Nine

Culp's Hill

As the Union line collapsed on the afternoon of the first day of fighting, they retreated through the buildings of Gettysburg to the high ground of Cemetery Hill and adjoining Culps Hill. The high ground of Culps Hill became the anchor for the Union Right flank throughout the battle. It was the scene of some of the bloodiest fighting of the battle and more Southern blood would be shed in this area than at the entire First Battle of Manassas. Rebel killed and wounded in this area alone were in excess of 2,250 with over 200 captured. Federal losses were over 1,000 killed or wounded.

At the time of the battle, Culps Hill had open wooded slopes that aided the Union in defending their positions. The defense of the right flank of the Federal line fell to the Twelfth Corps under the command of Maj. General Henry W. Slocum. The unsung hero in the defense of the hill was Brigadier General George Greene, a 62 year old Rhode Islander in charge of the 3rd Brigade consisting of war hardened troops from New York State. A military veteran that had graduated second in his class from West Point, Greene had worked as a Civil Engineer prior to the war and fully understood the advantage of holding the high ground and building fortifications to protect his troops. Upon his arrival on the morning of July 2, he had his troops construct a strong breast work of trees and earth along the ridge of Culp's Hill in anticipation of the Confederate attack.

By 4:00 in the afternoon of July 2 the left flank of the Federal line in the vicinity of Little Round Top was being attacked by Longstreet's Confederate First Corps. As the defensive line selected by General Sickles for the Third Corps was beginning to break in the area of Emmittsburg Road and the Peach Orchard, General Meade began to order all available troops to the battle zone in the hopes of avoiding a total disaster. The Commanding General took the gamble that his right

Sections of the original earthen breast works that were constructed under the orders of General Greene can still be seen on Culps Hill. In the image below you can see the earthen mound as well as a soldier peering down the line of the earthen breast work.

flank was secure for the day and removed all but General Greens single brigade consisting of 1,424 men to hold Culps Hill. What Meade did not realize was that the Rebels noticed that the Federal troops were being removed from the hill. As a consequence, General Johnson's Division of 5,000 seasoned infantrymen were about to attempt to take over the real estate held by Greene's men. The undersized Brigade had to defend almost ½ mile of trenches and breast works against almost four to one odds.

Skirmishers from the 60th New York spotted the Confederates crossing Rock Creek at the base of Culp's Hill about 7:15 in the evening. Indecision and poor communication among the Rebel commanders delayed General Ewell from beginning the assault until dusk. As near darkness descended under the canopy of the trees, Johnson's Division began their assault up the hill toward the fortified Federals. General Greene's men held their fire until the southerners were within 100 feet; then opened with devastating musket fire causing the Rebels to fall back and regroup. The Confederates made four separate charges between 7:00 and 10:00 with the limited success of capturing a section of the Federal breast works near the area of Spangler Spring. As the fighting subsided near Little Round Top, Union troops began to return to Culp's Hill and reinforce the positions held by the vastly out manned defenders. They found a portion of the fortifications built by the Federals occupied by the attacking Confederates. By dawn the Union fortifications were fully manned and the troops were determined to retake the lost breastworks at first light in the morning.

As the Confederate plan of battle evolved on July 3, General Lee determined that his First Corps would attack the center of the Union line on Cemetery Hill and fighting would renew on Culps Hill to divert troops from the grand assault that would be known as Picketts charge. Unfortunately for the Southern cause, the grand charge would be delayed until afternoon, long after the fighting ended on Culps Hill.

Fighting commenced the morning of July 3 with a bombardment at 4:00am by Union artillery as the first step in retaking the lost section of the breastworks. The combination of the fortifications of earthen and timber berms combined with the advantage of the high ground proved to be too much for the Rebel troops. Heavy fighting continued as the Rebels made three separate charges up Culp's Hill with heavy losses. About 10:00 am General Ewell ordered the Confederates to withdraw from the area and the battle for Culps Hill ended, long before Picketts' epic charge. The slopes of the hill were covered with in excess of 2,500 southerners killed or wounded. Because of the foresight of General Greene in constructing fortifications, just over 1,000 Federal troops were killed or wounded. Just as the 20th Maine fought valiantly against overwhelming odds on the left flank of the Federal Line, a small group of soldiers from New York fought as bravely in holding the out-manned right flank. On July 3, a total of 22,000 soldiers fought a sustained battle lasting 7 hours in which over 1 million rounds were fired in a single day in the area of Culp's Hill. The entire area of Culp's Hill is the scene of heavy paranormal activity.

The form of a soldier peers from the woods toward the Union breast works on the crest of Culps Hill. This is the area of the Confederate attack on the evening of the second day of the battle and three separate attacks on July 3. When the fighting was over, approximately 2,500 Confederate soldiers were buried in mass graves throughout the woods. In 1863, this area was not heavily wooded as it is today, but open with large trees.

This photograph was taken at the 29th Pennsylvania Infantry monument at Culps Hill. Note the unusual orb with a stripe and a partial facial image with eyes and nose. This was one of the regiments that was pulled the second day to help save the Third Corps defensive line. They returned the night of July 2 to reclaim their original position on the hill. This is a very unusual size and shape for a spirit orb and I believe does a lot to support the arguments of my opening chapter.

A classic example of friends and neighbors fighting against each other occurred near Spangler Spring. As a border state, Maryland soldiers fought on both sides of the conflict. The 1st Maryland (CSA) successfully captured a part of the Union breast works on the night of July 2. As they tried to advance the next day, as a twist of fate, they were opposed by the 1st Maryland (USA) that had been formed from men of the Maryland Eastern Shore. Devastated by the Union fire, the southerners took 400 men into battle and had 174 killed or wounded. Colonel James Wallace of the Federal 1st Maryland wrote of the day, "The 1st Maryland Confederate Regiment met us and were cut to pieces. We sorrowfully gathered up many of our old friends and acquaintances and had them carefully and tenderly cared for."

In the years after the war, another dispute over monuments occurred between the survivors of the 1st Maryland USA and the 1st Maryland CSA. In order to erect a monument on the northern battle field, the southerners had to change their name to the 2nd Maryland to avoid any confusion between the two units. When you view the area today, you will see a monument to the 2nd Maryland, a regiment that never fought at Gettysburg. I am certainly glad the survivors managed to clear up any confusion over who fought where.

Among the participants mortally wounded in the charge of the 1st Maryland CSA was their canine mascot, Grace. In my experience on the battlefield, I have photographed multiple examples of animal spirits. One summer evening I was photographing in the vicinity of the charge of the 1st Maryland CSA and found what I believe to be one of the more interesting images in this book. Below you will see an orb with the clearly defined image of a dog that I believe to be the image of Grace.

Spangler's Spring was a naturally flowing spring that lies at the southern end of Culp's Hill and is the subject of paranormal activities. Union troops of the Twelfth Corps were first to occupy the area and constructed earthen works on the Knoll north of the spring site. When elements of the Twelfth Corps was ordered to the Peach Orchard on July 2 to reinforce the Third Corps of Dan Sickles, the earthworks were temporarily abandoned. Confederates under General Edward Johnson arrived in the area after nightfall and took control of a portion of the breast works as well the area surrounding the Spring. Johnson actually had advanced to within several hundred yards of the Baltimore Pike, the main Federal supply line. He never realized that he could have attacked the rear of the Union defensive position without opposition.

As the Twelfth Corps began its counter attack in the early morning hours of July 3 with an artillery barrage, the Spangler's Spring area became another one of the killing fields during the battle with charge

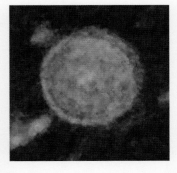

Taken near Spangler Spring, this orb shows the strong image of a dog, probably "Grace," still guarding her fallen comrades from the 1st Maryland regiment.

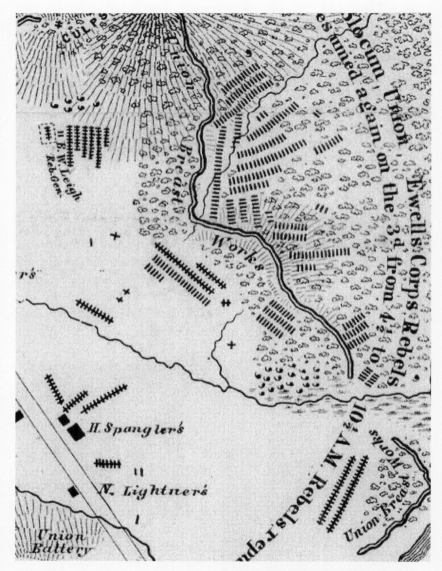

The Elliot map for the Culp's Hill and Spangler's Spring area shows the location of Rebel mass grave sites as well as the location of the Union defensive breast works. Over 2,000 Rebels were killed or wounded in this area. There is a definite relationship between the location of mass grave sites and areas of high paranormal activity.

An apparition stares from the woods.

A very unusual facial apparition appears in the area of the Union defensive line held by the Union Twelfth Corps.

The photograph above shows Spangler Spring surrounded by spirit orbs. Many other abnormalities have been seen near the Spring including a lady in white, supposedly a nurse that helped to attend to the dying and wounded. Another image seen in the area is "gray pants," the lower half of a Confederate soldier.

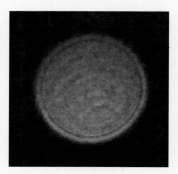

This large orb with a face was taken in the same area adjacent to Spangler Spring. You can see the partial face in the orb as it glows in the picture. Spangler Spring is one of the best known paranormal areas on the Gettysburg battle field.

and counter charge in the open meadows. Spangler's Spring is truly a place where the armies of both sides filled their canteens while participating in one of the bloodiest portions of the Battle of Gettysburg. Contrary to rumors, there was never a truce where they used the spring at the same time. At the time of the fighting, they really did not like each other.

An image taken near the area around Spangler's Spring, a soldier still looks out from behind the trees.

This is a classic example of the ghost hunter becoming the hunted. The following image was taken at the Indiana monument by my granddaughter on a warm summer night. As you can see, an unusual orb is quite curious about what happening with the old guy in the orange shirt taking pictures.

The action on Culps Hill played a large role in the outcome of the entire battle. A rebel victory here would have weakened the entire Federal defensive line and cut off the Union supply line. As you can see from the number of pictures in this chapter, spirits of the brave soldiers that fought here still want their story to be told.

A soldier peers from the trees near Spangler's Spring. This is the area where re-enactors are allowed to camp.

A cloud of ectoplasm in Spangler's Meadow.

Chapter Ten

The Peach Orchard

On the morning of the second day, General Meade instructed Major General Dan Sickles to position his Third Corps in a defensive line on Cemetery Ridge that anchored the Union left on Little Round Top and tied into the Second Corp along the ridge. One of the more colorful characters of the Civil War, Sickles had been elected to Congress in 1856. He was an ambitious part of the Tammany Hall political network and used his political connections to obtain power.

He drew national attention when he shot his wife's lover, who just happened to be Phillip Barton Key, (son of the composer of the "Star Spangled Banner"), to death across the street from the White House. His attorney in the trial was Edwin Stanton, soon to become Lincoln's Secretary of War. After a trial heavily covered by the press, Sickles was acquitted by claiming temporary insanity, the first individual to ever use that defense successfully. After being acquitted, he became a persona non grata among the elite of Washington. Perhaps the General's character can best be summed up in a quote George Templeton Strong, famous attorney and a founder of the U.S. Sanitary Commission, "One might as well try to spoil a rotten egg as to damage Dan's character."

Although he was not a West Point graduate, when war broke out the congressman raised a four regiment Brigade in New York City. As a reward for raising the unit, he was awarded the rank of Brig. General and placed in charge of the unit. The Brigade was assigned to the 3rd Corp under the command of General "Fighting" Joe Hooker. Sickles was a close friend of Hooker, and was promoted to Corps Commander as a result of the friendship when Hooker became Commander of the Army of the Potomac. Fighting Joe was the General that Meade had just replaced as Commander of the Army of the Potomac. It is a safe assumption that Sickles was not happy with Meade's promotion. General Meade also did not trust Sickles but the new Commander was given overall command only days earlier and there was no time for reorganization.

During the night of July 1, Meade and his generals devised a defensive plan which would fortify the high ground of Cemetery Ridge. Under this plan, the Third Corps would hold the ground between the Second Corps and anchor its flank on Little Round Top. Sickles spent most of the morning of July 2 worrying that the Confederates could batter his position from a ridge of high ground in front of Cemetery Ridge. In one of the most controversial moves of the battle, about noon time of the second day, General Sickles advanced his 10,000 men and artillery over half a mile from the Cemetery ridge defensive position ordered by General Meade. Because of the lack of manpower there was a 500 yard gap between the troops in the Peach Orchard and DeTrobrian's Brigade in the Wheatfield. By the end of the day his Corps would suffer over 4,100 casualties and Sickles would lose his leg to a cannon ball as a result of his decision.

The General felt that the higher ground at the Peach Orchard and area along the Emmitsburg Road would give Rebel artillery a decided advantage in the pending attack. As a result of the unauthorized repositioning of his Corps, a salient was created that could be attacked from multiple sides by the Army of Northern Virginia. Sickles was now forced to defend a line that was longer than could be defended by his two divisions.

General Meade was furious at Sickles who actually offered to pull his men back to Cemetery Ridge. Unfortunately, there was little he could do as the Confederate attack was imminent. Before the day ended, General Meade would send as many as 20,000 troops to reinforce the Third Corps in a futile attempt to defend their salient position. These troops would come from all parts of the battle field, including Culp's Hill. The redeployment by Sickles placed the entire Federal battle plan at risk and decimated his corps to the extent that it ceased to function as an effective fighting unit. Sickles, the ultimate politician, spent the rest of his life bragging that his brilliant movement of troops against Meade's orders had actually saved the Union from defeat.

General Longstreet was assigned the task of attacking the left flank of the Union line. In an effort to keep the movement of his troops hidden from the Union signal station on Little Round Top, Longstreet spent the entire morning getting his troops in position. As the Rebels organized for battle, the commanders were surprised to find the Third

A soldier standing behind the left gun still aims his cannon from the Third Corps artillery position along Wheatfield Road. I hope he wasn't aiming the cannon at the guy with the camera.

Corps in such an exposed position. The battle for the peach orchard began with an artillery barrage by Longstreet's 36 cannon that lasted for about 30 minutes. The barrage was quite punishing for the Union troops located in the Peach Orchard that could only wait for the oncoming attack. Union batteries on the Peach Orchard ridge and along Wheatfield Road replied with counter battery fire that also took a heavy toll on the Confederates.

General Sickles was wounded when a cannon ball struck his leg below the knee and his lower leg was left hanging by a thread. As he was being carried from the field, he had his staff light a cigar for him so his troops would not realize the gravity of his wound and keep up their morale. Sickles had his leg preserved in formaldehyde and his shin bone is still on display at the Smithsonian Institute. For the rest of his life, Sickles argued that his troop movement was a stroke of brilliance that assured the positive outcome of the battle for the North by disrupting Longstreet's assault. He was also the guy whose bust was left out of the Excelsior Brigade monument because he embezzled $30,000 from the monument fund. Some things never change with politicians; this guy could fit right in with our current crop in Washington DC.

Confederate units under command of General Lafayette McLaws, with the brigades of Barksdale and Kershaw in the lead, headed for the Peach Orchard and the Wheatfield. Union artillery opened fire on the advancing infantry using grape and canister with devastating effect. Early in the advance, a misunderstood command exposed the flank of

Sickles set his artillery on the edge of the Peach Orchard and along the Wheatfield Road. In this picture a soldier is still looking over the weapons that tried to stop the Rebel attack.

Kershaw's Brigade to the intense Union artillery fire creating many casualties. The entire area became a killing field as some of the fiercest fighting of the war was about to take place with thousands of dead and wounded. General Barksdale was mortally wounded while leading his troops in the assault.

General Meade immediately realized that the Third Corps could not hold off the massed rebel attack and ordered General Hancock to reinforce Sickles with a division from the Second Corps. Reinforcing

This 12-pdr. Napoleon fired canister into the oncoming Rebels. On the right side of the picture a spirit looks over the fence.

HAUNTING & HISTORY

theThird Corps left portions of Cemetery Ridge and Culp's Hill weak, creating more problems for General Meade as the day progressed. The ultimate collapse of Federal units on the Peach Orchard and Emmittsburg Pike would allow the Rebels to attack the flank of the troops attempting to defend the wheat field and force the Union line to basically where Meade had ordered it on the morning of July 2.

The carnage of the Peach Orchard, Emmittsburg Road, Wheatfield, Devils Den and Round Top would help make July 2, 1863, one of the deadliest days in American military history. General Sickles Corps had

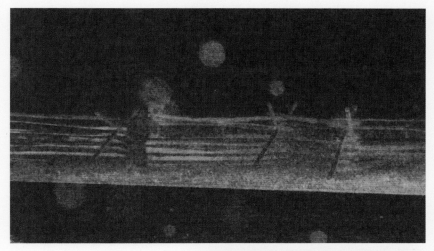

A full bodied apparition stands against the fence in the Peach Orchard. In the world of paranormal photography, this is about as vivid an image as you can take in the outdoors. Note the figure is wearing a top hat and a Lincoln type beard. The image is solid and you cannot see the fence through the apparition.

40% of the men who fought either killed or wounded. On July 3, it is probable that 5,500 Confederates and 7,800 Federal troops were killed or wounded in this area of the battle. Quite a feat considering the fighting lasted only about four hours. Only at the battle of Antietam would there be a more bloody single day in the American Civil War but on that day the fighting lasted over 8 hours.

On the left side of this image your will see a large, bright orb with a distinct face. The face in the orb seems to be looking at the apparition. Standing on the right there is a full bodied apparition. Note that the apparition is a solid mass and the rails of the fence cannot be seen behind the form. This is the fence that separates the Peach Orchard from the Rose Farm in the same area as the soldier on the preceding page. The photograph was taken in the area defended by the 141st Pennsylvania Infantry; one of the first positions of Sickle's extended defensive line to be overrun by the attacking Confederates. More than 60% of this unit was killed or wounded.

In one of the strange coincidences of the battle, John Wentz and his wife lived in a log home just north of Wheatfield Road and east of the Emmittsburg Road. Now in his seventies, Went decided not to flee his home but to stay in the cellar for safety. Their son Henry moved to Virginia 24 years earlier and returned to Gettysburg as a sergeant in Taylor's Confederate artillery battery. His battery was one of those that fired on the Peach Orchard and actually set up on high ground near the Emmitsburg Road in the vicinity of the Wentz house to fire at the Federal troops in retreat toward Cemetery Hill. When the fighting slowed, Henry found his father, whom he had not seen for 24 years, in the basement of his childhood home, unscathed from the fighting. That had to be a very strange reunion.

The Confederate onslaught drove the Federal troops back to their defensive line on Cemetery Ridge; the same place General Meade had placed them in the morning. The arrival of the 13,000 man Sixth Corps in the early afternoon after their forced march of 35 miles would save the day for the North. Cemetery ridge was now bolstered by the largest Corps in the Army of the Potomac under the command of General John Sedgwick. The exhausted Rebels were in no shape to take on the reinforced Federal line. Both armies held their positions in this area on July 3 as the grand assault tried to penetrate the center of the Federal line on Cemetery Ridge. Since the southern army held this area for a day after the fighting, it is safe to assume that the Rebels would have buried many of their own dead in unmarked graves. There is a high probability that many of the brave souls still remain in the ground of Gettysburg.

Full bodied apparitions in solid form as seen in this chapter represent some of the rarest images in paranormal photography. In my personal experience the odds of getting such an image is in the vicinity of 5,000 to 1. The casual visitor to the battlefield should not be disappointed if they fail to get similar images. The carnage and death in this area of the battlefield has produced some of the most amazing photography in this book, but I spent many months to get these results.

Chapter Eleven

The Wheatfield

On the afternoon of the second day, the wheatfield of farmer Rose was about to become a 19-acre killing field. The Wheatfield is situated between Devils Den and the Peach Orchard, with Trostle's Woods bordering it on the northern edge. Rose's Woods is on the south side and a part of Rose's Woods known as the Stoney Hill on the western edge. Little Round Top overlooks the area and lies to the east. At the height of the fighting, bodies of the dead and wounded would be stacked on each other to provide protection from the intense musket fire. By night fall there were 2,800 Confederate and 4,100 union casualties in this small area. Included in the dead were Confederate General Paul Semmes and Union General Samuel Zook. Survivors of the Wheatfield described the fighting as a surging whirlwind of death as the field changed hands many times in a period of several hours.

When General Sickles repositioned his Third Corps without orders from General Meade, he placed DeTrobriand's 1,500-man brigade in a defensive line that ran from Devil's Den to Stoney Hill. The 17th Maine was placed behind a stone wall at the southern end of the field on the edge of Rose's Woods, facing southward. They were the first to be engaged by Georgia and Arkansas regiments under the command of General George T. Anderson, attacking through Rose's woods. In fierce fighting, the 17th Maine held the line for almost an hour, being forced to retreat only when their ammunition was exhausted. In an attempt to stop the Rebels, as the unit grudgingly gave ground, General David Birney led the 17th Maine in a desperate bayonet charge that drove Anderson's men back to the area of the stone wall and resulted in fierce hand to hand combat. Overwhelming southern force drove the Federal troops back through the Wheatfield once again, with heavy loss of life. This stone wall on the edge of Rose's woods is an area of very active paranormal activity.

Fierce hand to hand fighting took place at the stone wall on the edge of Rose's Woods as the 17th Maine held off the advancing Confederates. In this picture, a soldier peers over the wall as a large orb can be seen by the tree in the center of the image.

The arrival of General Kershaw's Brigade of South Carolina troops from the direction of Rose's farm house forced Union General Barnes to order the withdraw of troops from the area of Stoney Hill. The retreat of two brigades to Trostle's woods created a gap in the Union line

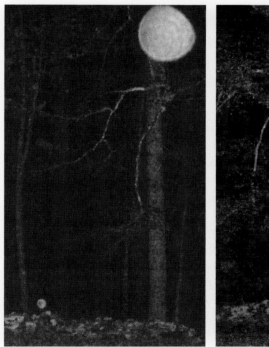 

Both of the above pictures were taken at the stone wall facing Rose's Woods. In the picture on the left a figure peers over the stone wall while a large orb appears in the upper right of the image. In the picture on the right, a figure is seen looking from the woods on the left while a face can be seen peering from the ectoplasm cloud in the upper center.

that was quickly filled by Confederates. Remaining units of DeTrobriand's men were now forced to retreat and the Wheatfield which was now in Southern hands. All of Sickles Corps was now driven from their lines.

Several faces peer over the stone wall that separates Rose's Woods from the Wheatfield as a group of orbs also keep watch.

The wall at Rose's Woods is among the most active paranormal areas of the National Park. Here, a face peers over the brush behind the wall. During the battle, this area was did not have the thick under brush that is present today. After the battle this area contained over 1,000 Confederate graves. Even though the bodies were disinterred in the 1870s, it is probable that some of the bodies were never discovered.

General Meade rushed a division consisting of four brigades from the Second corps to the Wheatfield to rescue the Third Corps from certain disaster, leaving Culp's Hill and portions of the Cemetery Ridge defensive line weak. Three brigades commanded by Patrick Kelly (the Irish Brigade), Samuel Zook and Edward Cross moved forward and cleared the Confederates from the Wheatfield with heavy loss of life. Losses to the Irish Brigade were so great they would cease to exist as an effective fighting unit. Colonel Zook was mortally injured in the fight to retake the wheatfield.

A battery of six Napoleons from the 19th New York, commanded by Captain George Winslow, was placed on a small rise to support the infantry. This unit was the only artillery directly supporting the action in the wheatfield. Winslow's Battery sustained heavy losses because of its close proximity to the action. As the Union lines collapsed on his right flank, Winslow would be forced to withdraw his battery from the field. The monument to the New York Light Artillery is the source of several outstanding paranormal pictures in this book.

A final counter attack, launched by the Union Fifth Corps under Gen. Samuel Crawford drove the Rebels, now exhausted from a long day of fighting, back across the Wheatfield and as far as the Stoney Hill. Crawford realized his troops were too extended and pulled them back to the eastern edge of the wheatfield. At the end of the day, more

An orb with a distinct face at the position of the 19th NY Artillery.

The full bodied apparition of a soldier stands in the Wheatfield.

than 20,000 men were engaged in the fight. Over 40% of the men that participated in this part of the battle were killed, wounded or captured and the Third Corps had been decimated.

The Elliott map of mass grave sites in the area of the wheatfield shows the location of some of the burial sites that blanketed the entire field. Since Rebel troops held this area on July 3, it is probable that they buried many of their own dead in unmarked graves. Although most of the bodies were moved to graves below the Mason-Dixon Line or re-buried in National Cemeteries, the spirits of many of the dead remain in the areas where they fell.

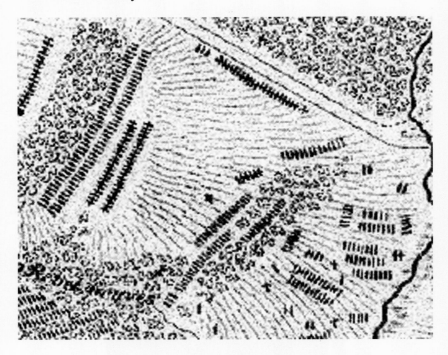

The Wheatfield is unquestionably one of the more spiritual areas on the Gettysburg battlefield. One warm summer night I was taking some friends out for an evening of paranormal photography. On this particular evening, there was no one else parked in the pull off area in the center of the wheatfield. My wife Connie decided she was tired and remained in the truck while we took pictures by the Pennsylvania Volunteers monument. On the way back to the truck I took the image on the next page and realized that she had a very special visitor. An orb was on the rear window of the truck and you could make out facial features looking toward her in the vehicle. Connie had actually been aware of his presence as she noticed a temperature drop across the top of her lap as she sat inside the vehicle. It is not uncommon to record temperature drops of as much as 10 degrees in the vicinity of active spirits. In this case the spirit must have actually been in the vehicle with her. I guess after 150 years his curiosity was aroused. I appropriately named this picture "Company for Connie."

In the world of paranormal photography, you often find subject matter that is totally unexplainable. The sequence of pictures on the next page was taken one fall night at the 19th New York Artillery monument looking toward the Stoney Hill. I have absolutely no explanation for the activity in the pictures. One possible explanation is that the object may be a light emitting orb moving very rapidly. The tree line in the photographs was about 200 yards away and the objects were inside the tree line. As you can see, the monument and cannon are in clear focus so I am not shaking the camera. I recorded eight frames of this activity that night. This is the only time I have photographed images of this nature.

In our paranormal investigations we rely heavily on a clairvoyant to communicate with and pass on information about the spirits. One night while near the 148th Pennsylvania Infantry monument the medium communicated with a Federal soldier. In the picture on page 89, you can see an orb with facial features in close proximity to the medium as she converses with the spirit presence.

She asked the soldier why he is still at the battlefield and has not moved on. His sad reply was that his brother fought in the battle and he

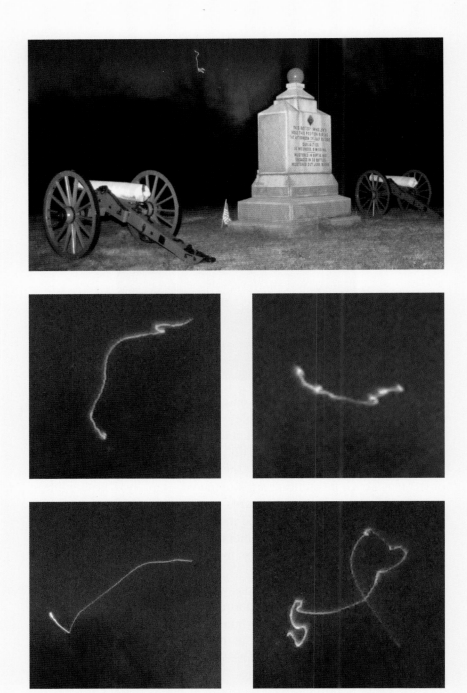

is remaining to find out what happened to him. Unfinished business seems to be a major reason for spirits to remain for long periods of time, in this case almost 150 years.

The wheat field of John Rose was the scene of unimaginable suffering and death. It remains the scene of remarkable paranormal activity as the spirits continue to celebrate the brave deeds of the soldiers of the north and south that met on a hot July afternoon.

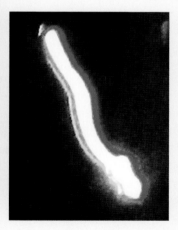

This very unusual moving mass was photographed at the Wheatfield. Please note the statue is in clear focus precluding any movement of the camera. I have no idea what is appearing in this image.

Chapter Twelve

Irish Brigade at the Wheatfield

ARGUABLY one of the finest and bravest fighting units of the Federal Army was the Irish Brigade. Formally known as the 2nd Brigade, 1st Division of the Second Corps under the command of General Winfield Hancock. Consisting of the 63rd New York, 69th New York, 88th New York, 28th Massachusetts and 116th Pennsylvania, the Brigade consisted mainly of Irish men recruited from the slum areas of New York. Formed as a fighting force of 5,000 men at the breakout of hostilities, nearly two years of war and especially the Battle of Fredericksburg had depleted the Brigade to 530 combat ready troops by July 1, 1863. These men were led by Colonel Patrick Kelley. Around 5:00 pm on July 2, with southern units in control of the wheatfield, the Irish Brigade was ordered from their position on Cemetery Hill to assist the beleaguered Third Corps.

Father William Corby was a Catholic priest attending to religious needs of the brigade. He had followed the troops giving spiritual leadership as well as comfort to the dead and dying since the beginning of the war. Knowing the soldiers were in for the fight of their lives and many would not return, he stood upon a rock and gave absolution and blessings to the hundreds of troops kneeling around him. He ended his blessing with what is now a famous quote, "The Catholic Church refuses Christian burial to the soldier who turns his back upon the foe or deserts his flag." With those words, the troops rushed off to one of the bloodiest struggles of the battle. After the war, Father Corby became the president of Notre Dame University. When Father Corby died in 1897 he was given a military funeral complete with a flag draped coffin and a rifle volley as he was being lowered into the ground.

In a hard fought advance, the Irish Brigade was able to clear the wheatfield of Rebels and take position on a rocky ridge. Unable to hold the position when support on their flank gave way, the brigade was

The statue honoring Father Corby stands on the same rock from which he gave his blessing assuring an eternity in Hell for cowards or deserters in the Irish Brigade. A bright orb is still paying close attention to his words. The Priest was nominated for a Medal of Honor for his bravery in comforting the wounded in the heat of battle.

forced to retreat. After suffering over 200 casualties in the wheatfield, the brigade was disbanded, no longer a functioning unit after this battle.

Located at the point of their farthest advance, one of the most distinctive monuments of the entire battlefield, a Celtic cross with an Irish Wolf Hound on the base, was dedicated in 1888. I can assure you that this is one of the most spiritual areas of the entire battlefield. It is the scene of one of my most memorable photographs as well as one my unforgettable paranormal experiences.

I was taking pictures one warm, fall evening in 2009 when I saw a re-enactor walking across the Wheatfield with a full size regimental flag of the Irish Brigade. After assuring myself that he was in fact real,

The Irish Brigade advanced to the base of the Stoney Hill under heavy musket fire. Unable to hold this position when the Union line broke on their right flank, they were forced to retreat. This picture shows the clear image of a face peering through the fence toward what would have been the advancing line of Kershaw's Brigade of South Carolina troops.

Pictured on the left is the regimental flag of the Irish Brigade. This is a replica of the flag described on the next page that was used as a trigger device at the Celtic Cross.

I struck up a conversation and asked him if I could use the flag as a trigger device for a couple of pictures.

We took the flag and draped it across the Celtic Cross monument. The image below is one of my most memorable portraits showing their reaction as they see their regimental flag for the first time in 150 years.

To the right of the Celtic Cross you will find three soldiers lined up as if stanting at attention, paying respect to the flag of the Irish Brigade. There is also a bright orb in front of the flag.

On another very dark evening last fall I arrived on the Wheatfield to find myself alone; or so I thought. Thinking to myself it was a perfect night; dark, quiet and no one else to disrupt my investigation, I headed to the Celtic Cross to take some pictures. After snapping a few frames, I became aware that there was a rustling noise, similar to the sound of a person walking, coming from the leaves behind me in the woods. Turning toward the sound, I took several pictures but could not see any images on the back screen of my cameras. I went back to taking pictures of the Cross. After a few frames, I again heard the sound of someone walking in the woods behind me. Pulling out a very large flash light, and now starting to feel a little uneasy, nothing could be seen in the lights path. Turning back to the monument, I took a few more pictures. Suddenly behind me I heard the long stride sound of walking in the leaves but this time there was also the sound of a twig breaking. Whatever was making the sound in the woods wasn't visible in the flash light but also had enough weight to break a twig. At times like this, discretion is the better part of valor and I got out of there as fast as my aging body would go.

On a another occasion in August, 2010 my wife and I were leaving the Devils Den area to go and stopped by the Celtic Cross monument to grab a few pictures before the park closed for the night. It was getting late in the evening. There were no other cars in the area and no one was near the monument. I parked the truck in the exact spot where I heard

A soldier peers through the bushes at the Celtic Cross. This monument marks the spot where the Irish Brigade fought on the second day of the battle.

the footsteps the year before, rolled down the window and took a picture through the truck window. Suddenly there is a lound crack as an object struck the right rear panel of the truck; the sound of a small stone striking metal. Luckily there were no park rangers near as we left the area at a high rate of speed. I went back the next day in daylight to investigate the scene and make sure there was no logical explanation for the event. There was indeed a small stone lying on the black top road at the exact location of our unnerving experience the night before.

Sometimes I am a very slow learner and now my curiosity was really aroused. Two weeks later I asked the medium to come along and find out what was happening when I tried to take photographs in the area of the cross. I did not mention what had transpired in the past, only that I had witnessed some strange activity. When we walked up to the area of the cross she approached me, looked me directly in the eye and said "they really don't want you here." She did not elaborate any additional information. Although incidents like this are rare, there are definitely areas where spirits are less than fond of the attention and have ways of letting you know it.

It is my opinion that the flash of the camera reminds the spirits of the flash of a musket muzzle. Armies of the period feared night fighting because there was no way to tell who was the enemy and who was friendly. Perhaps the best example of friendly fire was the shooting of Stonewall Jackson in the dark at Chancellorsville. On many occassions the first picture taken with flash will have orbs and the next picture will be clear of any activity as the spirits seem to flee from the sudden flash of light. Perhaps the spirits at the Celtic Cross are especially sensitive to light and respond accordingly to the rapid sequence of flash from my photographic equipment. Maybe they don't like me because I am not Irish (even though I do like Irish whiskey). Whatever the explanation, I have taken my last flash picture in the vicinity of the Celtic Cross.

Chapter Thirteen

Triangular Field

As late afternoon arrived on the second day of fighting, troops were finally in position on both sides for a collision course with destiny. Houck's Ridge ended at Devil's Den where the Union troops of the Third Corps awaited the onslaught of Longstreet's battle hardened troops. The 4th New York Battery commanded by Captain James Smith was positioned atop Devils Den, overlooking a patch of land that became known as the Triangular Field. Smith was only able to place four of his six Parrot rifles on top of the hill. Likewise, there was no room for his caissons because of the large boulders on the crest of the high ground. With his caissons below the crest of the hill, each round had to be carried by hand up the slope to the guns. Initial protection of the artillery fell to the 4th Maine who positioned themselves behind the stone wall below the battery. The 124th New York, known as the "Orange Blossoms," remained in line in the rear, out of sight of the advancing enemy.

Opposing the Union line would be seasoned troops from Georgia and Texas under the direct command of one of the South's most experienced commanders, General John Bell Hood. As the Rebel line began its attack, a shell exploded over the head of General Hood, badly injuring his left arm. He would lose permanent use of his arm as a result of the exploding shell. Smith's battery is credited with firing the shot that injured General Hood. This loss delayed the attack as chain of command shifted to Brigadier General Evander Law who at first did not realize he was in charge of the Division. Without decisive command structure, some of the Confederate regiments became misdirected in their attack and hurt the efficiency of the Rebel advance.

Smith's Battery changed to canister as the 1st Texas approached Rose Run at the base of the Triangular Field and inflicting heavy damage on the Texans. When the Rebels were within 30 yards of the crest of the hill, Major James Cromwell called for his horse and personally led a bayonet charge by the Orange Blossoms against the advancing Texans. The attack caught the Rebels by surprise and drove the southern infantry to the lower stone wall and momentarily shifted the momentum of the struggle. Major Cromwell was mortally wounded in this charge.

The Rebels reorganized at the relative safety of a stone wall at the base of the triangular field. Smith's battery now could not depress the cannon barrels enough to fire on the southerners at the stone wall. The battery continued to fire on the second wave of advancing Rebels under command of General Benning.

The 1st Texas began to advance again toward Smith's Battery. When they had advanced half way up the field, the 124th NY fixed bayonets, stood up from their hidden position and fired on the unsuspecting Confederates. The Rebels held firm and continued to advance toward the upper stone wall intent on capturing Smith's four Parrott rifled cannon.

About this time General Benning's Confederate Brigade began to arrive and fired a devastating volley into the New York infantry. As a result, the remaining New York officers were killed and the Orange Blossoms in the Triangular Field were leaderless. Smith ordered a withdrawal from the crest of the hill leaving his guns as a prize for the advancing Rebels. As the Confederates advanced they surrounded and took many Federal prisoners. The battle for triangular field came slowly

Smith's Battery was captured by Rebel troops on the second day after inflicting heavy casualties on the advancing Texans. This shadow figure still mans the guns.

to a bloody end. When the Rebels took control of the high ground they came under Union cannon and sharpshooter fire from Little Round Top.

Failure of the Union forces in the Peach Orchard and overwhelming assaults along the Union Third Corps positions carried the day and Smith's Battery was captured by the forces in gray. When the battle began, the New York "Orange Blossom Brigade" defending the high ground near Devils Den numbered 1,500. By nightfall, the unit was decimated with the loss of 46 officers and 712 enlisted men. Confederate losses were similar in numbers. As many as 2,000 men were casualties of war in this relatively small area known as the Triangular Field.

The carnage in Triangular Field sets the stage for incredible paranormal activities. This is one of the best known locations to paranormal investigators. Cameras malfunction, strange sounds and voices can be heard while a creepy feeling persists when walking through the field. I was once in the presence of a sensitive child who could repeat the words spoken by the voices of soldiers who were still responding to their orders. Once I was challenged by the words "Who goes there" when there was no one else in the area. Several years ago the National Park Service removed trees in the area of Triangle Field to make it appear more like it looked at the time of the battle.

The following sequence of pictures shows the evolution of an ectoplasm cloud culminating in a vortex shape. This amazing sequence was taken during a time frame of 20 seconds in Triangle Field approximately 50 yards below the upper rock wall fought over by both sides. It was taken on multiple cameras that were fired in a rapid sequence with flash. Amazingly, I could not see any of the activity with my eyes as it was happening, but I could observe the formation of the cloud on the back screens of my cameras. Yes, as the cloud evolved about 10 feet in front of my camera I thought it might be time for a new hobby.

The first and second photos in the series show the initial formation of the paranormal phenomenon known as an ectoplasm cloud. In the second image it appears that a shape is in the center of the cloud.

In the third image in the series, the cloud begins to take a vortex form and grow in shape. The fourth picture shows a cloud that appears to be growing with orbs and shapes emerging within the mist.

The final image below shows a fully developed vortex shaped cloud of ectoplasm. It fills the entire frame and was not cropped. The next frame was clear as the cloud dissipated in a second. Some believe that vortex clouds are portals between dimensions. After the event ended, I was very happy to remain in the current dimension.

Although this area was the site of massive violence and loss of life, there are no monuments to be found in the Triangular Field. Furthermore, since the National Park Service removed many of the

Haunting & History

trees in the area, it really doesn't even look like much of a triangle. That being said, I can assure you that the area is incredibly active for the paranormal investigator.

A figure stares over the stone wall that separates Rose's Woods from the entrance to Triangular Field. On the second day of fighting, this was an area of extremely heavy casualties.

This picture of the Triangle Field was taken looking west toward Rose's woods. If you look closely, you can see the faces of at least 3 soldiers looking over the stone wall.

This shadow figure looks over the wall from Rose's Woods. From this position, the Rebels fired upon the New York Orange Blossom Regiment. By the end of July 2, Southern forces held this entire area as Federal troops were driven off to Little Round Top.

A huge field of orbs gather at the lower end of the Triangular Field.

The final image below was taken along the edge of the woods that borders the triangle field.

We've discussed this shape before in Chapters Four and Chapter Five. I saved it for the last part of this chapter so you wouldn't think I was totally nuts for as long as possible. Just for the record, I still think it is a fairy. Feel free to prove me wrong with your own pictures.

Chapter Fourteen

Little Round Top

A partially cleared hill rising approximately 150 feet above the Plumb Run Valley was about to become a very important piece of real estate on the afternoon of July 2. General Meade's original plans called for General Sickles with his Third Corps to replace the Twelfth Corps in positions on Little Round Top. The Twelfth Corps was removed to Culps Hill. As noon approached, General Meade assumed his orders were followed and Federal defensive line would run in a fish hook pattern from Culp's Hill to Little Round Top.

When Sickles moved his entire corps to the Peach Orchard-Devil's Den line against Meade's orders, he left Little Round Top undefended. Not only was Little Round Top undefended but there were significant gaps in the Third Corps line that could be exploited by the Rebels. In the tactics of the Civil War era, the side that controlled the high ground would control the battlefield.

About 4:00 in the afternoon, Confederate General Longstreet and his seasoned troops began an attack from Warfield Ridge in an attempt to roll up the Union left flank. General John Bell Hood's Division was made up of some of the most battle hardened troops from Texas and Alabama. Their brigade was under the direct command of General E. M. Law, a competent field leader. They were positioned on the Rebel right flank and had the direct assignment of capturing the hill. With the left flank of the Union Third Corps anchored in Devils Den, Little Round Top was left undefended. As the Rebel attack began, Little Round Top could have easily been captured by the advancing Southern infantry.

When General Meade realized that Sickles left Little Round Top undefended, he dispatched Brig. General Gouverneur K. Warren, Chief Engineer of his staff, to figure out how to deal with the rapidly deteriorating situation. As Warren arrived he immediately realized the Southern attack was imminent and sent his staff to find any help that was available in the area to defend the high ground.

The first available unit found by Warren was Col. Strong Vincent's brigade of four regiments. Vincent had orders to march toward the Peach Orchard in an attempt to reinforce Sickles' advanced line. Warren however, ordered him to rush his soldiers to the defense of Little Round Top. Arriving only 10 minutes before the Rebels, he placed his regiments around the hill, anchoring the left flank with the regiment under the command of Col. Joshua Lawrence Chamberlain, a college professor turned soldier. Chamberlain's 20th Maine would be supported by the 83rd Pennsylvania on his right. Chamberlain and his 385 men were given orders by Vincent that their position must be held at all costs. What was about to unfold would win Chamberlain the Medal of Honor and cost Strong Vincent his life.

The 15th and 47th Alabama regiments consisted of 644 riflemen under the command of Col. William Oates. After their exhausting march that included marching over Big Round Top, they charged the Federal position three times in 90 minutes attempting to flank the 20th Maine. When night fell, the 20th Maine would only have 200 troopers available for service. Chamberlain's regiment had fired over 15,000 rounds in

In this photo you can see the monument that marks the extreme Union right flank on Little Round Top that was defended by the 20th Maine. To the right of the monument you can see the apparition of a soldier peering over the stone wall that was erected by the defending Union troops.

repelling the Confederates in less than 2 hours and his troops were down to the last of their musket ammunition. Knowing there was little he could do to stop the next assault, Chamberlain made one of the most daring decisions of the battle and ordered his men to fix bayonets and charge directly toward the oncoming Alabamans.

The frontal bayonet attack caught the Rebels by surprise, repulsed their attack and resulted in the capture of 400 prisoners. Over 150 dead Rebels lay in front of the Union positions. Chamberlain survived two wounds on Little Round Top and would receive a serious life-threatening wound 11 months later at Petersburg, VA. Thinking he was going to die, Ulysses Grant promoted him to Brigadier General on the field. The Maine native survived to serve four terms as governor of Maine and the remaining years of his life as President of Bowdoin College. Thirty years later, Chamberlain would be awarded the Medal of Honor for his heroic stand on Little Round Top as he became one of the great heroes of the War and a force in Maine Politics in later life. His opponent, William Oates had an arm amputated at the battle of the Wilderness and serve seven terms as an Alabama Congressman and one term as Governor of the State.

While the 20th Maine was struggling to hold on to the left flank, the battle was not going well for the Federals along the rest of the line. Col. Strong Vincent had only 263 men to hold the remaining portion of the hill with the 44th New York and the 16th Michigan Regiments. While under strong assaults by the 4th and 5th Texas regiments, the 16th Michigan began to give way. Vincent was mortally injured as he rushed to encourage the Michigan regiment.

At the height of the fighting on Little Round Top, the 83rd Pennsylvania, positioned on the flank of the 20th Maine was holding their own against the advancing Rebels. The image on the top of the next page was taken in the vicinity of the defensive line of the 83rd and shows the presence of four shadow figures looking over the stone wall as well as an ecto mist presence in the right coner of the photograph.

Reinforcements arrived in the form of the 140th New York under the command of Patrick O'Rorke and a battery of 4 artillery pieces under the command of Charles Hazlett. The New Yorkers immediately charged the Texans with O'Rorke being killed in the assault. Amazingly, the cannon were maneuvered by hand to the top of the ridge but were of little help as Confederate marksmen pinned down the gun crews. Hazlett was killed by the Rebel marksmen. Because of the steep slope of the terrain, the gun crews could not depress their barrels enough to fire

Two soldiers look over the edge of the hill at the summit of Little Round Top.

Exhausted Texas troops tried to attack the Union positions on Little Round Top. This picture shows a soldier peering over the boulders that line the ridge of the hill. Federal troops fired from behind boulders and hastily erected stone breastworks upon the southern marksmen in Devils Den.

effective against the attacking Texans. The next day they directed effective fire against Pickett's Division in the grand assault.

Reinforcements from the Sixth Corps saved the day and the Texans were driven back to the area around Devils Den. Sharpshooters from both sides continued to add to the body count until night fall brought an end to the killing. During the night, Federal troops built up stone breastworks to defend themselves the next day from an anticipated attack that never materialized. Instead, the next day General Lee sent his troops against the middle of the line at Cemetery Hill in what is now known as Pickett's charge.

The arrival of the reinforcements of the Sixth Corps finally pushed the rebels from Little Round Top for the last time as darkness began to fall on the field of battle. Both sides continued sharpshooter fire on July 3 as Lee re focused his attention on the center of the Union line.

A figure peers through the brush toward the crest of Little Round Top. This is the area where the 140th New York drove the Texans down the hill as Col. O'Rorke was fatally injured.

This picture was taken looking toward the crest of Little Round Top as it would have been viewed by the Texas regiments. In the background you see the shape of the Pennsylvania monument. Although the entire picture shows the presence of spirit orbs, the head of an apparition can be seen looking over the boulder on the left side of the image.

Chapter Fifteen

Devil's Den, the Slaughter Pen & the Valley of Death

With the failure of General Sickles Third Corps to hold at the Peach Orchard, the subsequent collapse in the Wheatfield and the capture of Smith's Battery at the head of Triangular Field, the Confederates from Hood's Division swarmed into the boulders of Devils Den and the Plumb Run valley. Opposing them would be Union soldiers of the Fifth and Sixth Corps on Little Round Top and Cemetery Ridge. Once again control of the high ground by the Federal troops brought the Rebel advance to a halt as artillery and musket fire from the elevated positions would make southern advances untenable.

Union sharpshooters were the brainchild of Hiram Berdan who formed the units in 1861. His men dressed in distinctive green uniforms and fought independently. In order to qualify for the sharpshooters regiments the applicant had to hit a bullseye 10 consecutive times at a distance of 200 yards. Union sharpshooters had a killing range of up to 600 yards. Their specially designed Sharps rifles were equipped with double-set triggers and in some instances scopes to allow accurate fire at extreme distances. Devil's Den, Plumb Run valley and the Slaughter Pen were well within the killing range of the sharpshooters.

The low ground near Devil's Den holding the slow running Plumb Run became known as the Slaughter Pen as advancing Confederates were mowed down by Union fire. The boulders in the area caused confusion as the Rebels tried to hold their battle lines. The Plumb Run valley to the north of Devils Den would become known as the Valley of Death as the wounded and dying would crawl to the water to cleanse their wounds or take a final drink of water. Witness accounts say Plumb Run ran red with blood for almost 3 hours. This section offered little cover or protection for the Rebels from the rifle fire as Federal reinforcements rushed to Little Round Top.

Devil's Den is a bizarre outcropping of huge boulders that had a huge impact on the fight. Originally the left flank of the Third Corps line, continued attacks by Texas and Alabama infantry eventually captured Devil's Den and the Plumb Run valley. Union sharpshooters on Little Round Top took a huge toll of the Confederate soldiers, especially the Texas fighters in the Slaughter Pen. In response, Southern sharpshooters took control of the boulders in Devil's Den, planted the Confederate flag on the highest point and answered the Federal fire. Only nightfall stopped the killing as both sides practiced their deadly trade. The intense fire killed high ranking officers and infantry on both sides. Especially decimated were Union artillerymen unprotected as they reloaded the muzzles of the cannon on Little Round Top. Southern marksmen accounted for the deaths of Brig. General Stephen Weed, Col. Strong Vincent and Col. Patrick O'Rorke. Some Southerners among the boulders were killed by the concussion of shot and shell striking the stones. Survivors of the fighting described the outcropping of the boulders as the "Devils Hole." None of the soldiers that participated in the fighting would forget the living hell of the afternoon of July 2.

This picture taken in Devil's Den shows an ecto mist on the left, contrasted with a ground fog in the rest of the picture. Note the flash reflected from the water particles of the ground fog while there are no water particles present in the ectoplasm or ecto mist.

A large cloud of ecto mist appears in Devil's Den. I could not see this with my naked eyes, only in the camera.

The Plumb Run Valley between Devil's Den and the Round Tops earned the nickname "Slaughter Pen" on the afternoon of July 2. As the Texas and Alabama infantry drove the Union from Devil's Den and tried to attack the high ground of Little Round Top, they became easy targets for Union soldiers firing from hastily constructed stone breastworks on the high ground. Two of Smith's remaining artillery pieces were located in the north end of the valley to fire cannister at the advancing southerners. Late arriving cannon from the Sixth Corps added to the killing spree. In spite of their being easy targets, Rebel troops without artillery support repeatedly attempted to charge the high ground of Little Round Top. By the end of the day bodies covered the field. This entire area is the scene of active paranormal activity.

This picture was taken in the Slaughter Pen section of the Plumb Run Valley. Note the orb activity with an unusual light pattern. I have no clue as to the moving light. In the lower right there is a soldier peering through the brush.

In a photograph taken from the location of Smith's Battery, an ecto mist is accompanied by some strong images. The upper orb has a good facial image while a figure peers over the brush at the bottom of the picture. There are 3 facial images in this picture.

On the edge of Devil's Den, a light emitting orb seems to shoot from the ground itself. Note that the rock is in sharp focus as the orb seems to shoot toward the sky. The lens was probably open around 1/60 of a second.

This picture was taken in the portion of the Plumb Run Valley known as the Valley of Death. The apparition is in the center of the picture. You can see the beard of the soldier in the enlargement.

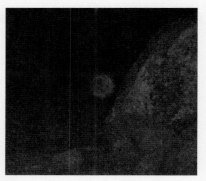

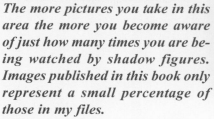

The more pictures you take in this area the more you become aware of just how many times you are being watched by shadow figures. Images published in this book only represent a small percentage of those in my files.

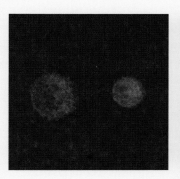 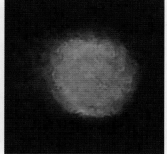

The picture above features two distinct facial images. It is quite unusual to find two strong faces in close proximity. If you are visiting the battlefield and feel like you are being watched, you probably are!

Chapter Sixteen

Cemetery Ridge Defensive Line

L<small>ATE</small> in the night the first day of fighting, General Meade met with his Generals to attempt to find reason from the chaos of the day. The Confederates had driven them back to the high ground overlooking Gettysburg, forcing them to consolidate their men and artillery into a small area. Meade determined that they would set up a defensive line on the high ground of Cemetery Ridge, await reinforcements, and let the Confederates make the next move. The new commander was a topographical engineer and his knowledge and use of terrain proved to be a huge factor in the outcome of the battle. When General Sickles moved his Third Corps, without orders, about noon of July 2, the plan of battle changed drastically.

About 6:30 on July 2, Confederate forces were overwhelming the Federal line along the Emmitsburg Road and the Peach Orchard. When Sickles was wounded, General Hancock took charge of the debacle sending in reinforcements to make the best of a bad situation. Brig. General Wilcox's Alabama Brigade was approaching the base of Cemetery Ridge and had delayed to reorganize for the assault. About 500 yards from the copse of trees that was to become the focal point of the grand assault the next day, there was a gaping hole in the Union line guarded only by an artillery battery and their infantry support, the 1st Minnesota.

General Hancock became aware of the impending Rebel breakthrough and rode up to the regimental commander, Col. William Colville. The closest reinforcements were ¼ mile away and closing rapidly but Hancock realized he had only one hope of avoiding a major breach of his line. He looked at Colville, pointed toward the first Rebel flag that was quickly approaching and shouted "Take those colors." With only 262 men, the undersized regiment fixed bayonets and charged into the oncoming Alabama troops. The Minnesotans faced a force totaling over 1,000 men knew there would only be one outcome. The Alabamans were momentarily halted by the brave Minnesotans as their bayonet charge bought enough time for other Union regiments to reinforce the area. As a result of this act of incredible bravery, the 1st Minnesota suffered the highest casualty rate, 81%, of any Federal unit at Gettysburg. As the Federal reinforcements arrived, Wilcox had no support and ordered his troops to retreat toward Seminary Ridge. The sacrifice of the 1st Minnesota saved the Cemetery Ridge line.

The monument to the 1st Minnesotta depicts an infantry soldier charging toward the enemy. A large neon orb seems to be encouraging the soldier toward his appointment with destiny.

Adjacent to the Minnesota monument a figure peers from the grass toward the supporting artillery battery.

The deepest penetration of Rebel troops actually occurred on the afternoon of the second day. As Wilcox was retreating with his troops, Anderson's third brigade under General Ambrose Wright advanced against Cemetery Ridge about 400 yards from the copse of trees. Amazingly, Wright found a seam in the defense and drove to the crest of the Ridge. The General recorded in his battle report that he could see Federal supply wagons on Baltimore Pike. In one of the great missed moments for the Confederacy, he had the opportunity to split the Federal defenses but did not have enough men to exploit the breach. The two remaining brigades of Anderson's Division, under Generals Posey and Mahone, had not advanced in support of the attack. Wright ordered his units to retreat rather than risk his men being cut off by the arriving Union reinforcements. General Lee thought the success of Wright proved the weakness of the Union center and Wright's success was one of the factors that contributed to the his decision to direct the Grand Assault against the center of the Federal line on July 3.

On the morning of July 2, General John Sedgwick's Union Sixth Corps awoke in Manchester, Md. at 4:00 am to orders for a double quick march to join the battle at Gettysburg, 35 miles away. Consisting of approximately 20,000 men and 40 artillery pieces, the "Fighting Sixth" executed one of the most exhausting forced marches of the war. They arrived at Gettysburg by 4:00 in the afternoon, just in time to reinforce Little Round Top and stop the Rebel advance through Devil's Den and the Wheatfield. They maintained an average rate of almost 4 miles per hour in temperatures reaching 90 degrees!

A cloud of ecto-mist seems to cover the body of a fallen soldier at the New York Light Artillery monument on Cemetery Ridge.

Upon reaching the battlefield, a battery was immediately placed upon the high ground around Little Round Top to assist the beleaguered Fifth Corps and began firing upon the Rebel troops below. Accounts of soldiers fighting here report the activation of the artillery was a huge morale boost to the Union troops that were at that time being driven back in defeat. The Sixth Corps actually fired few shots in the battle, but their overwhelming presence stopped the Rebel advance.

In one of the great "what ifs" of the battle, had General Longstreet not been delayed with his counter march, his troops would have carried the field of battle before reinforcements could have arrived in the form of the Sixth Corps. The loss of the left flank at Little Round Top would have altered the entire engagement at Gettysburg.

In the image above you can see the plaque to the 3rd Brigade with a cloud of ectoplasm in the upper right hand corner of the picture. If you look closely at the enlarged insert you will see the eyes and face of a figure looking from the cloud of ectoplasm.

The 3rd Brigade of the Sixth Corps, as well as the 3rd Mass. Artillery was placed in an advanced line at the base of Cemetery Ridge close to Plumb Run at the end of what was to become known as the Valley of Death. The following picture was taken there.

Taken in the same area as the ectoplasm in the preceding photo, an orb on the rock in the left portion of the picture shows a strong image of the spirit.

By late in the fighting of the second day, exhaustion and dehydration were taking its toll on both sides. The Rebels had been marching all morning in the intense heat just to get in position to engage the enemy. The Sixth Corps was the largest corps in the Army of the Potomac and the sight of their regimental flags appearing on Cemetery Ridge was a huge deterrant to the southern commanders. General Sedgwick placed his troops in a very strong defensive line on Cemetery Ridge abutting Little Round Top. His presence controlled this part of the field for the remainder of the battle.

While the Sixth Corps had a relatively small number of men actively engaged in the fighting, its presence had a huge bearing on the outcome of the battle.

Located along the line of battle for the Sixth Corps near Plumb Run on the end of the Valley of Death, the 3rd Mass. Artillery was positioned to fire upon the oncoming Rebels from the Wheatfield. This unique series of photographs is taken approximately two seconds apart and shows a cloud of orbs surrounding the battery. The next frame, taken two seconds later, shows no activity in the area of the cannon.

Chapter Seventeen

Pickett's Charge

As the sun rose on July 3, General Robert E. Lee knew that after the two days of carnage, his exhausted troops had enough energy and ammunition for one more day of aggressive fighting. The Rebels did not have the luxury of supply wagons from the South to restock shot and shell. Heavy losses had depleted some of his key fighting units as well as high ranking commanders. Major General George Pickett and his division from Virginia were the last to arrive, had not seen action during the first two days, and were well rested. No general ever had more confidence in the fighting ability of his troops than General Robert E. Lee. Unfortunately for the South, this confidence would lead to an afternoon in Pennsylvania that would be the turning point of the war and lead the way to a Union victory two years later.

After two days of fighting, Confederate troops had been to some extent successful, but had been unable to capture the Union positions, now heavily fortified on Cemetery Ridge. Lee devised a plan to attack the center of the Federal line. He felt that heavy fighting on both flanks forced reinforcements to be sent to those areas, weakening the middle. The southern commander sent three divisions under the command of General James Longstreet, consisting of approximately 12,500 men in a charge across one mile of open fields. They would strike the center of the Union line. General Longstreet voiced strong opposition to the plan but in the end followed the orders of General Lee.

General Lee had the following plan of battle for the third day:

1. Maj. General Edward Johnson was to attack Culp's Hill, the right flank of the Union Line. This attack should act as a diversion and force General Meade to take troops from the real point of attack.

2. In the middle of the line, at the planned point of attack, a huge artillery barrage would preceed the infantry attack. This bar-

rage was expected to destroy the Union guns and weaken the Union infantry positions at the point of attack.

3. According to Lee's plan, Confederate calvary under J.E.B. Stuart would move around the Union right flank and attack the rear of the Union line. The confusion created should also break the Union supply lines along Baltimore Pike.

4. After the artillery barrage and concurrent with the two diversionary actions, General Longstreet would make a direct assault on the Federal position running along the crest of Cemetery Hill. The Southern troops would concentrate on a clump of trees that became known as the High Water Mark of the Rebellion.

Things went wrong with Lee's battle plan from the beginning. Orders were never sent to Pickett's Division to be in place for an early morning assault. It was almost noon until the troops were in position for the attack and the artillery barrage did not begin until 1:00 pm.

On the right flank of the Union line, the Federal artillery barrage began at 4:00 a.m., forcing an early start to the engagement. General Johnson began a 7 hour battle for Culp's Hill that resulted in failure to overcome the Federal breastworks that were heavily reinforced by General Meade. About the time fighting ended at Culp's Hill with the Southern retreat in that area, the grand artillery barrage began from Seminary Ridge. The end of the fighting on Culp's Hill by mid day allowed troops to be diverted back to defend the assault at the Angle.

As Southern troops withdrew from Culp's Hill, three brigades of Confederate cavalry, numbering approximately 3,400 men, were confronted by Union cavalry at East Calvary Field. The Federal cavalry numbering 3,250 troopers was commanded by Maj. Gen. Alfred Pleasanton and Brig. Gen. George Armstrong Custer. The cavalry battle began at the same time as the great Confederate barrage at Seminary Ridge. In a short but violent battle Union troops succeeded in stopping the Confederates in their tracks. Northern losses numbered 254 casualties with southern losses reported at 181. Confederate hopes of attacking the Federal rear and disrupting supply lines were stopped. The attack of Stuart's cavalry did not contribute to the success of the grand assault as hoped for by General Lee.

The key to the southern infantry being able to penetrate the Union line on Cemetery Ridge was in the hands the artillery. A line of over 140 cannon stretched almost six miles in length along Seminary Ridge. The idea was to wrap the artillery around the Union position so shells could be lobbed into the center of the line from three sides. Fifty-six guns were kept to the rear as a reserve to be moved where needed. These artillery reserves were never committed during the bombardment, one of many command errors made during the battle. Counting the reserve guns, Lee had almost 45 guns per mile facing the Federal line.

Another problem haunted the Rebel gun crews; poor quality of powder and fuses. The length of the fuse would determine when the projectile would explode in the air, covering the area with deadly shrapnel.

Southern fuses by this time of the war were notoriously unpredictable. It is estimated that many of the fuses malfunctioned during the bombardment sending the shells harmlessly over the heads of the Union soldiers without exploding. With the Northern positions hidden by the smoke of battle, Southern commanders did not realize that the infantry would be charging positions not weakened by the artillery fire.

Facing the Rebel onslaught was entrenched Federal artillery along the high ground of Cemetery Ridge. With the arrival of the Sixth Corps, General Meade commanded a huge assortment of heavy armament that would put a staggering 120 guns per mile to face the Army of Northern Virginia. The high ground of the Northern positions gave a huge advantage to the gunners, especially those positioned on Little Round Top. Commanded by General Henry Hunt, a brilliant artillery commander, the guns were well positioned with sufficient reserve ammunition. At the end of the day, Union guns only used 50% of the shot and powder available in contrast to the Confederates expending most of their available ammunition.

One of the greatest bombardments of the war was under the command of Col. Edward Porter Alexander. Alexander was a graduate of West Point and a brilliant artillerist but had only commanded at the battery level prior to Gettysburg. On the morning of July 2, General Longstreet placed him in command of his artillery, replacing James Walton. Alexander performed well but the lack of experience at the Corps level would result in units being held in reserve when they should have been assisting in the attack. Longstreet actually gave Alexander the discretion to have Pickett begin the attack when he felt the bombardment had reached its desired results. Amazingly, the grand assault would begin at the discretion of a colonel, not a general. At 1:00 in the afternoon the artillery bombardment, the greatest of the war, began with the firing of two signal shots. As if an omen of what was about to happen, one of the fuses on the signal shot would not fire and the second signal shot was delayed until the fuse was changed. The thunderous sound of cannon fire was heard over 100 miles away.

Union counter battery fire delayed for approximately 15 minutes to conserve ammunition. General Hunt wanted to hold return fire until the Rebel infantry formed into battle lines and became easy targets. Under the urging of General Hancock, the Federal batteries along Cemetery Ridge returned fire and the battle began in earnest. After about 30 minutes, General Henry Hunt ordered one of the grand deceptions of the battle. He had his cannons to slowly cease fire. This maneuver created the illusion that the batteries were being destroyed by the Confederate fire. Blinded by the smoke, the Confederate generals believed the Union cannon had been silenced. They had actually been repositioned to conserve ammunition and await the anticipated attack. Thinking the Union batteries were silenced, Col. Alexander, the officer in charge of the Southern batteries, sent word to General Longstreet that if the attack was to begin it must begin now as the Confederate artillery was running out of ammunition.

General Longstreet, realizing the futile nature of the attack was overcome with emotion and merely nodded his approval for General Pickett to begin the assault. Nine brigades numbering around 12,500 men in a line of battle a mile long emerged from the woods of Seminary Ridge and began the assault on the Federal line. General Pickett's Division of Virginians was on the right, with the brigades of General Pettigrew in the middle and General Trimble on the left. The advance was met immediately with Union artillery fire from the entire length of Cemetery Ridge and from the heights of Little Round Top. Round shot would hit in front of the advancing line and act like bowling balls as the exploding shot overhead rained shrapnel on the advancing Rebels. As the line of battle came within 400 yards of the Northern breastworks, the fire turned from ball and solid shot to double canister and musket fire. The devastating combination stopped Pettigrew's Brigades on the left flank of the attack at the Emmitsburg Road.

In addition to the murderous cannon fire on the Confederate left flank, there was yet another unanticipated blow to the Rebel attack. On July 2 when Longstreet's Corps was attempting to roll up the Union flank, General Meade placed the 8th Ohio regiment in a defensive position west of the Emmitsburg Pike, about 300 yards in front of the main line of Union breastworks. Imagine the sinking feeling in their stomachs when over 12,000 Confederates came out of the Seminary Ridge woods line and it looked as if their regiment was the first to feel the full brunt of the attack! As the Rebels began to concentrate on the copse of trees, the 8th Ohio found their unit on the flank of the advancing Rebel

Soldiers peer from the grass near the position of the 8ᵗʰ Ohio and the Emmittsburg Pike.

Brigade commanded by Col. John Brockenbrough. With the aid of artillery fire from Ziglers Grove, the 8ᵗʰ Ohio poured a devastating fire into Brockenbrough's Brigade, causing them to break to the rear, creating confusion and weakening the entire flank of the charge. This was the first Southern unit to ever break and flee under General Lee's command. By the end of the day the Ohio Regiment collected around 300 prisoners of war.

The vast number of Confederate grave sites shown on the portion of the Elliott map on the next page hints that most of the men were killed in the vicinity of the Emmitsburg Road. It appears that Pettigrew's Brigade failed to cross the road, most of the graves of his brigade were on the west side of the road. Perhaps the most devastating blow to Lee's battle plan occurred at the Emmitsburg Road. On each side of the road there was a stout rail fence that had been placed there by the farmers. The attacking rebels actually sent squads of men in front of the infantry battle lines to knock down the fences but they were unable to remove them in their entirety.

The infantry was also unable to knock down the heavy fences at the Emmittsburg Road and had to climb over both fence lines under murderous fire from musket and artillery. They were like sitting ducks for the Union infantry behind the breastworks several hundred yards away. Union troops had even collected the weapons of the dead and wounded to use as additional fire power.

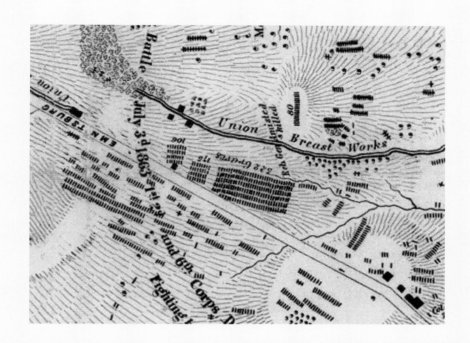

The National Park Service has done a good job in having the area appear as it did on the day of Pickett's Charge. Seen here is the fence along the Emmitsburg Road with a group of spirit orbs. This is the area of the stout fence rows and mass Rebel grave sites.

A cloud of ecto mist is seen dissipating in the area of Pickett's Charge where General Armistead and a small group of Confederates crossed the stone wall.

The Angle is marked by two large trees and boulders. This soldier looks over the boulders toward what would have been the most heavily fortified portion of the Federal line.

On the Confederate right, remnants of Armistead's Brigade, 200 men strong, actually crossed the stone fence at the Angle. Reinforcements were rushed to the area by General Meade and the attack was contained with Confederate General Armistead being mortally wounded. In less than an hour, the hopes of a Southern victory were destroyed as the South could never rebuild from the losses of Gettysburg.

History records Pickett's Charge as a blood bath of epic proportions. Total Rebel losses during the attack were 6,555 casualties, over 50% of the men present at the beginning of the attack. Pickett's three brigade commanders and all thirteen of his regimental commanders were casualties. The loss of General Armistead was mourned on both sides. Union reports indicate that almost 3,800 Rebels were captured. Federal losses were approximately 1,500 men killed or wounded.

One company of the 11th Mississippi Infantry, known as the "University Grays" participated in the grand assault. When war broke out, around 110 students at the University of Mississippi enlisted in the army and were accepted as Company A of the 11th Regiment. By July 3, 1863, only 31 members of the "Grays" answered the call for duty. Decimated by Union fire they fought their way to the Brian Barn in the vicinity of Zigler's Grove. By the time they reached the barn, eight color bearers of the 11th Mississippi were shot down before the shaft of the flag was cut by a minnie ball. Only a handful of the regiment fought their way back to Seminary Ridge.

The Confederate attack on July 3, 1863 was one of the most famous and controversial military actions in the annals of history. It was an act of incredible bravery for the nine brigades that participated in the charge. They crossed almost 1 mile of open field under heavy bombardment, climbed two fences, charged into the face of horrific canister and musket fire in 90 degree temperatures. It is amazing that any of the men involved in the charge lived to cross the stone wall and stand on ground that is now known as the high water mark of the Rebellion.

The Rebels crossed almost a mile of open field between Seminary Ridge and the Union breastworks on Cemetery Ridge. This soldier looks toward the Union line from near the Emmitsburg Road and the wooden fences that delayed the charge.

Chapter Eighteen

The High Water Mark

A small grove of trees on the northern portion of Cemetery Ridge is known in history as the "High Water Mark of the Rebellion." The spot of the northern-most penetration of Rebel forces in actual combat is marked by a monument of an open book propped up on a pyramid of cannon balls that was dedicated in 1892. Pages of the book bear the names of commands of both armies that participated in Lee's grand assault. It marks the spot of vicious hand to hand fighting that ended Southern hopes for a victory on Northern soil and ultimately any opportunity to negotiate a truce acceptable to the South.

Attacking Rebels were given orders to concentrate on the copse of trees that Lee felt would be the weakest area of the Union line. Defense at the center of the attack fell to the Second Corps under command of Major General Hancock, one of the best Federal commanders. Around the copse of trees the Philadelphia Brigade, commanded by Brig. General Alexander Webb, was entrenched behind a stone wall.

The area of Cemetery Ridge selected by General Lee for the main assault featured a stone wall below the crest of the hill that jutted out to form an angle; then ran back near the crest of the hill to Zigler's Grove. The men had collected the muskets of their fallen comrades that they stacked and loaded so more firepower could be exerted without taking time to reload their weapons. Battery A of the 4th NY Artillery, positioned just north of the clump of trees, was commanded by Lt. Alonzo Cushing. Since this area was the concentration point for the upcoming attack, his battery was the focus of the Confederate bombardment. By the time of the attack his battery was reduced to two usable cannon. During the bombardment Cushing was injured by shell fragments and although he was in great pain, continued to command his battery, directing return fire.

As the infantry attack began, Cushing received permission from General Hancock to move his two remaining cannon to the stone wall.

He loaded them with double canister and fired point blank into the advancing Virginians. As he fired his remaining gun, the Lieutenant fell to a Rebel bullet in the mouth and died instantly at the height of the attack.

In the vicinity of Zigler's Grove north of the angle, two brigades of the Second Corps commanded by General Alexander Hays were firmly entrenched behind a stone wall. They were supported by artillery placed on higher ground at the edge of the trees. Opposing Hays were troops commanded by General Pettigrew and General Trimble both of whom were wounded in the assault. Artillery from Cemetery Hill and Zigler's Grove had a devastating effect on the brigades commanded by Pettigrew and Trimble. These batteries held their fire during the Rebel bombardment incurring considerable damage and only fired when the oncoming Southern infantry was in the open fields.

Intense Union shot and canister as well as enfilading fire from the 8th Ohio broke parts of Pettigrew's battle lines. The routing of his men would disrupt the flank of Trimble's troops. As Pettigrew's men were

A residual haunting can be a visual image attributed to a traumatic life-altering event. This rare image shows the barrel of a ghost cannon situated above a 12-pdr. Napoleon at Zigler's Grove. Note that the upper image of the barrel is a larger size than the real cannon. The image of a soldier looks on from the left side.

fleeing toward the relative safety of Seminary Ridge, Trimble's men began to follow suit. General Pettigrew was painfully wounded in the hand and Trimble in the leg during the fighting. When the battle ended, Hays' men found over 2,500 muskets discarded in front of their position. In addition, his division captured 15 battle flags. The 108th New York infantry regiment was positioned in Zigler's Grove to support the 1st US Artillery. In this area the Confederates advanced to within 50 feet of their line before breaking under the withering fire. The 108th New York sustained 102 casualties of the 200 men engaged.

Fighting the Union troops at the Angle were the mingled remnants of Pickett and Pettigrew led by General Lewis Armistead. The Rebel general had been a cadet at West Point and was a good friend of Union General Hancock. Armistead was expelled from West Point in 1836 for hitting Jubal Early over the head with a plate, perhaps an indication of things to come. He had served in the regular army with distinction and chose to fight with the Southern cause. As the Virginians approached the wall under withering fire, Armistead rallied approximately 200 soldiers, placed his hat on the tip of his sword and led the men over the wall shouting "Give them cold steel." They overran several Union cannon before Armistead was mortally wounded as he laid his hand on one of the captured cannons.

A cloud of ecto mist dissapates near the stone wall at the angle.

General Armistead was killed as he placed his hand upon a captured cannon. This image shows the monument where Armistead was killed with a large orb presence.

In one of the coincidences of the battle, Union General Hancock and Confederate General Armistead, best of friends but on opposite sides, were both wounded at approximately the same time. Armistead, a Mason, gave a Masonic distress signal when he was mortally wounded. Witnessing the distress call, a Union Captain who was also a mason, went to his aid. Armistead told Capt. Bingham of his special relationship with Hancock and asked that his personal effects be given to him. The Captain carried out the Southern general's wishes and his belongings were passed on to his old friend. General Hancock was seriously wounded when a bullet hit his saddle driving a nail into his leg but survived as one of the heroes of the battle.

Union reinforcements poured into the area and the Rebels would have no one to reinforce their hard gained positions. Ohio and Vermont regiments directed withering musket fire on the flanks of the attack. Any remaining southerners were either killed or captured. The Rebel troops withdrew from the field leaving their dead and wounded in the hands of the victorious Federal troops. Union soldiers cheered "Fredericksburg, Fredericksburg" as a payback for a previous Northern disaster. When General Lee asked Picket to rally his division to prepare for a potential Union counter attack, his reply was "General, I have no Division." Forty-two regiments took part in the initial attack of which twenty-eight had their colors captured by the Federal troops. The South had never suffered this type of defeat since the war began and the idea of Confederate invincibility was shattered forever.

A soldier peers over the stone wall above the angle. This is the same location as the ecto mist appeared (two photos previous).

The Federal Second Corps commanded by General Hancock bore the brunt of much of the Rebel Grand Assault. This Second Corps monument east of the High Water Mark is being guarded by a rapidly moving, light emitting orb. The entire area is a source of intense spirit activity.

When the battle was over, the task of burial of the Confederate dead fell to the Union soldiers. The remains of 1,242 Southerners were buried along the Second Corps front in long trench graves, among them the body of a female dressed in a Confederate uniform. It is believed that the wife of one of the Rebel soldiers posed as a soldier and accompanied her husband on the assault where they were both killed.

By the end of July 3, 1863, Southern hopes for a victory on northern soil were dashed. Lee had lost 1/3 of his famed Army of Northern Virginia and would never again have the supplies or ammunition for a major assault on the North. The city of Vicksburg fell on the same day as Pickett's Charge and there would only be dark days ahead for the Confederacy as the war would linger on for 2 more years. Two months later General Lee offered his resignation to President Jefferson Davis but the resignation was not accepted.

By the 1880s the different veterans' groups were raising money for monuments to mark the spot where their units had seen action. The 72nd Pennsylvania sued to place their monument at the stone wall and their case went all the way to the Pennsylvania Supreme Court. They actually purchased land in front of the wall and threatened to place the monument on their own land. Not all the fighting took place between the North and the South as northerners tried to grab the glory of the victory.

Some of the most intense fighting of the Grand Assault occurred in this area in the vicinity of the High Water Mark. This cloud of ecto mist seems to hang in air like the smoke and dust of the battle itself.

A large monument marks the position of the 71st Pa. Infantry at the Angle. In this picture a figure peers from around the monument toward the Union defensive line. This is one of the most active areas on the battlefield.

The entire area of the Angle and High Water Mark is a source of great paranormal activity. When photographing in this area it is quite common to experience very short battery life in your cameras, as the spirits draw on the energy of the batteries. One night while photographing in this area I was forced to change the batteries in my cameras six different times. My cameras seemed to go dead (pardon the pun) at the most active times.

Monument to the 72nd Pennsylvania is situated at the stone wall. This image shows orbs of various colors as well as a cloud of ecto mist.

Chapter Nineteen

East Cavalry Field

For the first two years of the war, Confederate cavalry proved to be invincible against the mounted troopers of the North. In the agrarian society of the South, horses were an integral part of their way of life. Youngsters learned to ride at an early age and these skills were inherent to the ability of the Rebel cavalry in the early years of the war. In the North, the more industrialized culture did not rely as heavily on horses and the riding skills had to be learned by Federal cavalry. Two years of war provided on the job training and by the middle of 1863 the mounted troopers of the north were approaching the skill level of their Southern counterparts.

Several weeks earlier, Union cavalry had fought the famous Rebel cavalry to a standoff at Brandy Station. They had successfully surprised and almost captured Stuart himself during the battle. For the first time southern newspapers criticized Stuart for allowing a near defeat. Union cavalry considered Brandy Station as a victory, since this was the first time the southern horse soldiers were stopped in their tracks. The taste of defeat was not pleasant for the flamboyant general and he fully intended to make up for his poor showing on his next raid.

In the Confederate Army, each trooper supplied his own horse. As a result, if you lost your animal, it could be quite a while until another mount was found. In many instances, a skilled rider would be delegated to infantry since no mount was available or he could not afford another one. The loss of horses resulted in a degradation of available Confederate cavalry. Northern cavalry was provided with their mounts and equipment so the loss of a horse would have no effect on the availability of manpower. In addition, Federal mounted troops were provided with the latest weaponry in the form of breechloading carbines. Confederate cavalry weapons were generally muzzle loading carbines. In close fighting, both sides relied on pistols and sabers.

The famed southern cavalry was led by 30 year old J.E.B. Stuart, a flamboyant leader whose success had captured the imagination of the citizens of both the North and the South. General Lee had complete confidence in Stuart and relied heavily upon him for intelligence information. At the beginning of the Northern invasion, Lee had Stuart embark on a raid around the flank of the Army of the Potomac intending to have him join up with Ewell's Corps in their attempt to capture Harrisburg, PA. Stuart was specifically instructed by Lee to keep within courier contact throughout the flanking movement. When Stuart lost complete contact with Lee, the commander was deprived of the information that the Army of the Potomac was moving north under General Meade, the new commander.

As Stuart carried out his raid, he was plagued by bad luck from the start. Early in the raid he captured 150 supply wagons as well as a large number of prisoners near the town of Rockville, MD. These wagons and the accompanying prisoners would create havoc in his efforts to make progress in the attempt to link up with Ewell's Corps. To make matters worse, as he approached the town of Hanover, PA, Union cavalry was waiting for the invaders. Stuart himself avoided capture when he was forced to jump a 15 foot ravine on his horse. Unable to defeat the Federal troops at Hanover, he was forced to sneak around their positions at night, further adding to the delay.

In his attempt to find Ewell's Corps, he continued his forced ride north to Carlisle. Ewell had left the town 12 hours earlier when his Corps was recalled to Cashtown to reinforce General Lee and concentrate forces to face General Meade. The final blow for his men was the 31 mile ride from Carlisle to join Lee in Gettysburg. By the time they arrived, his troops and animals were in poor fighting condition. The eight day raid where they covered at least 210 miles had been exhausting and a severe test for man and animal alike. They would have only a few hours of rest before being asked to face Union cavalry on July 3.

Stuart and his four brigades of cavalry did not arrive in Gettysburg until late in the afternoon of July 2, too late to play any role in the fighting of the first two days. When he finally met with General Lee, the commander rebuked him for not providing the critical information concerning the location of the Army of the Potomac. Stuart's command originally consisting of 6,000 men was reduced to approximately 3,400 troopers and 13 pieces of artillery.

The cavalry's arrival gave General Lee the opportunity to carry out his planned frontal assault led by Pickett's Division. Mounted troops had the ability to attack around the Union right flank that was entrenched on Culp's Hill. The desired effect of the flanking assault by the cavalry on Meade's rear positions was the disruption of lines of supply from Baltimore and Washington. In addition, Federal troops could not be moved to help defend against Picketts coordinated assault on the middle of the line. Stuart would also control the Baltimore Pike, the main supply route for Meade's Army. If the Grand Assault was successful, Stuart could cut off Meade's retreat route and the defeat of the Army of the Potomac was assured.

Awaiting the Southern cavalry were troops under the command of Maj. General Alfred Pleasonton. Confidence of the Union cavalry was never higher since they had recently been victorious at Brandy Station, the only bright spot for the North following Chancellorsville. Immediately in Stuart's path was the division of Brig. General David Gregg. His command was supported by the "Michigan Brigade" under the command of 22 year old General George Armstrong Custer who had just been promoted to Brig. General. Custer had finished last in his class at West Point but had proven to be one of the best Union fighting commanders. Custer's Brigade was armed with Spencer repeating rifles, a huge advantage over the weapons of Rebel cavalry which could only fire a single shot. Altogether there were 3,250 Union troops to oppose the attack of Stuart.

Stuart began his attack by firing signal shots with his cannon to let Lee know he was beginning his assault. Unfortunately for the South the shots also alerted General Plesanton of the presence of Stuart. The Southern cavalry began with an artillery barrage but Union counter battery fire got the best of the early fighting. About the same time as the barrage began against Cemetery Ridge in advance of Pickett's Charge, troops under Fitz Hugh Lee scattered Union skirmishers in front of the Federal line with a direct attack. Union General Gregg answered with a counter attack lead personally by Custer and his Michigan regiments. Shouting "Come on Wolveriners." Custer and his men eventually drove back the Confederates. General Stuart answered with reinforcements that broke Custer's pursuit and forced their retreat.

Sensing a weakness, Stuart tried again for a breakthrough by sending in Wade Hampton's Brigade of experienced troopers, arguably the best unit in the southern cavalry. Union batteries tried to stop the advance but Hampton's Brigade was able to avoid the cannon fire. Custer once again led a counter attack with his 1st Michigan Brigade that culminated in both sides colliding at full speed with horses crushing riders

At the base of this monument on East Cavalry Field is a light emitting orb or object. Another orb is seen on the left side of the monument. This marks the area where the main fighting occurred and therefore the spot of the most casualties.

and hand to hand combat. With Custer fully engaged, Union reinforcements assaulted the Confederates from three sides. During the vicious fighting Custer had another mount, his charger "Roanoke" stumble, throwing the young general to the ground and forcing him to finish the fight on a horse that was made riderless in the fighting. Wade Hampton had to withdraw from the battle with saber cuts to his head. After heavy losses on both sides, the famed southern cavalry was forced to retreat. Union cavalry was exhausted from the intense encounter and were unable to pursue the retreating rebels.

The encounter at East Cavalry Field only lasted for about two hours of intense fighting with 254 Union casualties, 219 of them from Custer's Michigan Brigade. Confederate losses were reported at 181 but were probably understated. Custer himself had two horses shot out from under him during the height of the action. In spite of the Union losses being greater than those of the south, this was a strategic loss for the Southern cause. Lee's hope for a strike against the rear of the Union line was foiled and troops would not be diverted from the defense on the grand assault by Pickett. Neither Stuart nor Pickett would be able to carry their objectives. Also shattered was the reputation of superiority for the famed Confederate cavalry. Federal horsemen had met the best mounted troops of the Confederacy and had proven victorious. J.E.B. Stuart's reputation as the dashing and unbeatable cavalry cavalier would

Another photograph at the cavalry monument shows a
spirit soldier peering from the brush adjacent to the monument.

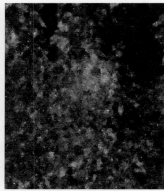

A ghost dog peers through the woods near the cavalry monument. Note the similarity with the ghost dog photographed at East Cemetery Hill in Chapter Seven.

be tarnished as would be the hopes for a southern victory on northern soil. The only official rebuke by Lee would be statement in his official report that his troops were "embarrassed" by the lack of information supplied by the cavalry.

For most visitors to Gettysburg, East Calvary Field is often overlooked as part of the battlefield tour. The area of the Confederate Calvary charge and the Gregg Calvary Shaft is quite active with paranormal activity.

A light emitting orb goes by the 7th Michigan Cavalry monument on East Cavalry Field. This was the unit commanded by General George Armstrong Custer. If you look closely at the right edge of the picture you can see the face of a soldier peering through the corn field.

Chapter Twenty

South Cavalry Field

Most tourists that come to Gettysburg have no clue as to what events took place at South Cavalry Field. As the fighting of the second day engulfed the Peach Orchard, Wheatfield, Devil's Den and Little Round Top, Maj. General Alfred Pleasanton, Meade's cavalry commander, was ordered to guard the left flank of the Federal line. Two brigades under the control of General Gregg were posted south of the Rock Creek Bridge along the Baltimore Pike. These units engaged General Stuart at what is now East Cavalry Field. Brigadier General Hugh "Kill Cavalry" Kilpatrick was ordered to take his two brigades south along the Baltimore Pike to the village of Two Taverns. The 27 year old Kilpatrick had graduated from West Point in 1861 and had only assumed division command on June 28. Hungry for action and glory, the young General had faced Stuart at Hanover on June 30 and Hunterstown on July 2. On July 3, Kilpatrick lived up to his nickname, Kill Cavalry.

As the third day of fighting began, Southern forces held a line that stretched from the base of Big Round Top, through Devil's Den in a rough line through the Slyder and Currens properties, crossing Emmitsburg Pike and extending to Seminary Ridge. These were the same units that defeated Sickles' Corps and faced Chamberlain on Little Round Top. Exhausted but still full of fight, they dug in behind fence rows and fortified their positions. South Carolina and Georgia regiments were positioned west of the Emmittsburg Pike and troops from Texas and Alabama were positioned east of the road to the base of Big Round Top.

On the morning of July 3, Kilpatrick received orders from Pleasanton to move his remaining two brigades northward and attack the Confederate flank. He was to be joined by General Wesley Merritt's Reserve Brigade that was coming north from the town of Emmitsburg. A second order arrived from Pleasanton sending one of Kilpatrick's brigades under the command of General George Armstrong Custer to join Gregg in defending the Federal flank near the intersection of Low Dutch Road and the Hanover Pike. General Kill-calvary believed the new orders weakened his forces and were issued by mistake. General Custer definitely benefited from the change of orders. Had he stayed with Kilpatrick, he might have missed his appointment at the Little Big Horn.

Kilpatrick was left with a single brigade consisting of approximately 1,900 officers and men from Pennsylvania, West Virginia and Vermont. These men were commanded by Elon Farnsworth who had just been promoted from Captain to Brigadier General 5 days earlier. His rapid rise in command may have had something to do with the fact that he was the nephew of an important Congressman. Promotions like that were known to happen in the Union Army. The Farnsworth House Restaurant in Gettysburg is named after the young general. In spite of how he may have gotten the promotion, he died bravely as a hero at Gettysburg.

About 1:00 pm, concurrent with the grand bombardment raging prior to Pickett's Charge, Kilpatrick's Brigade arrived and positioned themselves on slightly elevated ground named Bushman's Hill, near the base of Big Round Top. They could see the entrenched Confederates from Texas and Alabama north of their position. The terrain separating the two armies was lightly wooded, broken with high fencing and boulder outcroppings. Fighting an entrenched army over this type of terrain would be extremely difficult for mounted cavalry. Since the fences were too high for the horses to jump, the soldiers would have to dismount and tear them down under enemy fire. Kilpatrick's Brigade waited for the arrival of Merritt, listening to the deafening sound of battle as Pickett's assault was repulsed by the center of the Federal line.

Merritt began the engagement by sending in the 6th Pennsylvania, fighting dismounted against the South Carolina and Georgia Confederates. The 6th Pennsylvania had a unique history in that it was issued European style long lances at the beginning of the war. It did not take long for them to realize that lances were ineffective against muskets and artillery fire. By this point of the war they were armed with carbines and actually fought dismounted in this engagement. The entrenched veteran Georgia troops had little trouble repulsing Merritt's troops west of and along the Emmittsburg Pike. Things took a decided turn for the worse when the inexperienced Kilpatrick ordered Farnsworth to make a mounted attack across the highly unfavorable terrain. Farnsworth thought the order was a mistake and immediately realized

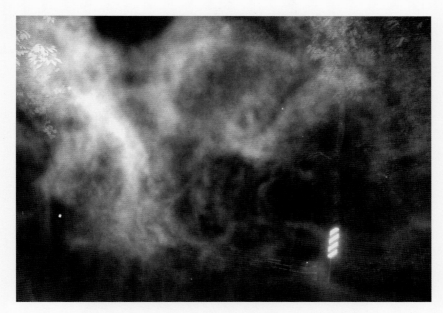

Just past the monument featuring Major Wells on Sykes Avenue, is the bridge over Plum Run. In this photograph you can see a huge cloud of ecto mist. The yellow is a reflector placed by the National Park Service to keep tourists from running into the bridge. Although overlooked by other paranormal investigators, South Cavalry Field is a place with very strong activity.

that he was being ordered on a suicide mission. Kilpatrick was hungry for fame and glory and was determined to get into the action.

After a discussion with his subordinates, Farnsworth approached Kilpatrick and tried to talk him out of the mounted attack. According to accounts, Kilpatrick countered by challenging Farnsworth's bravery and threatened to lead the charge himself. Farnsworth allegedly replied "General, if you order the charge I will lead it, but you must take the awful responsibility." With that comment, he rode off and organized his men for the assault. The 400 man 1st West Virginia Cavalry led the attack. After sustaining heavy fire they retreated, leaving 98 casualties. Next to go in was the 18th Pennsylvania supported by the 5th New York. They were driven back leaving 20 casualties on the field.

Last to go in was the 1st Vermont Cavalry, led by General Farnsworth with 400 officers and men. They fought their way to the Slyder Farm where the general had his horse shot out from under him. A corporal gave him his horse and he continued to lead the men to safety by heading toward the base of Big Round Top. As he neared the 84th Alabama they fired a volley; General Farnsworth was struck by 5 bullets and mortally injured. Major William Wells, now in command of the survivors, would be awarded the Medal of Honor for leading the troops to safety as the Alabamans continued their withering fire. Nothing was accomplished by the loss of life and horses, as the next day the Southerners began their retreat back to Virginia.

After Gettysburg, Killpatrick continued as commander of the Third Division until the spring of 1864 when he devised a disastrous raid on Richmond. When the popular General, Ulrich Dahlgren was killed on this raid Sherman transferred him to finish the war fighting in the West. The battle at South Cavalry Field contributed noth-

I have no clue what the image is in this picture. It was taken on South Cavalry Field on June 12, 2011.

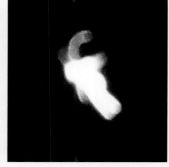

ing to the Federal success at Gettysburg. Judson (Kill-Cavalry) Kilpatrick is remembered as ordering a charge that marks a low point in the annals of American cavalry history. Most visitors drive through this area on the way to Little Round without realizing the heroics and useless loss of life that took place there or the active paranormal activity. The monument to Elon Farnsworth stands near where he fell, a victim of Alabama marksmen.

I took this image about 50 frames later and 300 yards from the previous image. It looks like the same "whatever it is" taken above.

In this image an unidentified flying object moves toward the camera as a soldier watches from the grass.

Chapter Twenty-One

Sach's Bridge

FOLLOWING the disastrous charge of July 3, what remained of Pickett's Division retreated to the relative safety of Seminary Ridge and attempted to prepare for a counter attack by Meade. On July 4 the sky opened up with a drenching rain that brought operations to a halt. Both armies stayed in place on July 4 and waited to see what the other had in mind. General Meade decided against any aggressive counter attack. His inability to deliver a death blow to the Rebels angered President Lincoln and the general was heavily criticized for not pursuing the retreating Army of Northern Virginia. General Lee realized that his army had neither the ammunition nor the healthy manpower to continue his invasion of the North. He ordered Longstreet's heavily damaged Corps to begin the retreat into Maryland and on to the safety of Virginia.

The resulting wagon train, filled with as many as 10,000 wounded and dying soldiers, stretched for miles. In addition, when the Army of Northern Virginia left Pennsylvania, they abandoned as many as 7,000 wounded soldiers to be cared for by the Federal doctors. Every house, barn, tavern and even open fields became makeshift hospitals as the Union doctors also had as many as 15,000 of their own to care for.

As the Rebel First Corps began their exodus from Gettysburg, they traveled over a wooden bridge that crossed Marsh Creek. Originally constructed in 1852 by William Stoner, the bridge was utilized by both sides for the movement of troops. There is a widely believed rumor that while the southerners were crossing the bridge during their retreat, three deserters were hung from the structure to serve as a grim lesson for anyone not willing to fulfill their duty. No historical evidence supports this claim. There are plenty of spirits on the bridge without the three deserters.

Some of the badly wounded were left at a home that was converted to a makeshift hospital near the bridge. Others that were mortally

An enlargement of the orb clearly shows the face of the spirit peering at the people on the bridge. The form of a woman has also been seen in this area.

wounded were simply left along the road to die. Many of the Rebel dead were buried in the fields surrounding the bridge in unmarked graves. It is believed that many of their remains were never disinterred and still remain in close proximity of the bridge, contributing to the intense spirit activity.

Sach's Bridge is regarded as one of the premier areas for paranormal occurrences and is considered one of the most haunted places in

This picture was taken from the approach to Sach's Bridge. This is the road taken by Pickett's Division while moving the wounded and dying soldiers south for medical care and approximately 300 yards from a structure that was used as a military hospital.

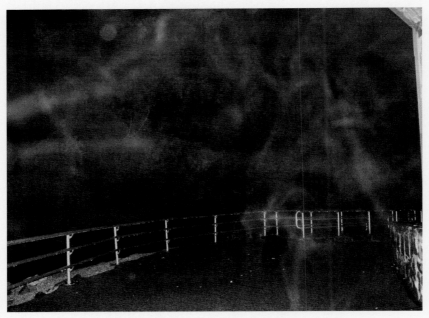

An ecto mist forms at the portal of the bridge.

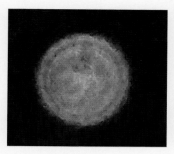

This picture from Sach's Bridge shows the image of a face looking out of what appears to be a round portal in the orb. This is the area of the bridge where three deserters were supposedly hung from the rafters during the retreat. I am pretty sure this guy isn't a deserter.

America. Pictured below is an orb that seems to be looking at the visitors to the bridge on a warm summer night.

In 1996 a flood tore the bridge off its foundation and washed it down Marsh Creek approximately 100 yards. The structure was rebuilt using 90% of the original materials. Spiritual activity does not appear to have been diminished by the re-building of the bridge.

A single bright orb takes up the center of Sach's Bridge.

A distinct face looks at the camera on Sach's Bridge.

Chapter Twenty-Two

After the Storm

JULY 4, 1863 was a day marked with a deluge of rain as if God was attempting to wipe clean an example of man's worst brutality toward another human being. Rain gauges in the town measured well over one inch of water. As many as 30,000 men, a number greater than the entire population of Adams County, were wounded and needed medical care. No planning or forethought was given to the care of the wounded after a major battle; after all, the battle came as a complete surprise to the participants. Since the Confederates were in full retreat to the safety of the south, they abandoned many of their wounded and had no time to bury their dead.

Each of the Federal Corps had surgeons assigned that would set up field hospitals and care for the immediate needs, such as amputation. (Doctors performed more than 60,000 amputations during the Civil War) There were 17 field hospitals set up by the Union and 18 by the Confederates during and immediately after the battle. In addition, most of the private homes, schools and churches took in the wounded. Many were cared for in fields and woods near water. On July 5, 1863 the Army of the Potomac made the first mention of establishing a hospital to care for the wounded. It fell to the medical director, surgeon Jonathan Letterman to appoint members of his command to comply with the orders. It was not until July 20, more than two weeks after the last shot was fired, that a large general hospital was established on York Road. The facility would be named Camp Letterman.

The job of organizing the dozens of field hospitals fell to Dr. Henry James, surgeon for U.S. Volunteers. The job of Dr. James and his staff was to move and consolidate the wounded that could not be moved into the facilities at the new general hospital camp. Anyone that could be moved was taken to the railroad depot and transported to permanent hospitals in large cities such as Baltimore and Washington, DC. Official records show that the total wounded handled by Dr. James was 20,995 with 14,193 being Union and 6,802 Confederate. A group of southern surgeons stayed to continue caring for their wounded, thinking they would be allowed to return to their units after their wounded were fit to travel. They cried foul when the surgeons were made prisoners of war. The Southern surgeons were moved to a prisoner of war camp as their reward for trying to do the right thing. Approximately 4,200 soldiers could not be transported because of their wounds and were moved to Camp Letterman.

The medical facility established in Gettysburg actually became a model for future facilities with clean and well managed care. At its peak, there were 400 tents placed in rows approximately 10 feet apart, each tent holding up to 10 patients. A medical officer was responsible for 40 to 70 wounded soldiers. Camp Letterman had operating tents, dining tents, quarters for staff and most of the facilities found in current aid stations. There was also a dead house, embalming tent and hospital graveyard. Union dead would be embalmed and sent to their families or temporally buried in the hospital graveyard. When General John Reynolds was killed on the first day of fighting, no embalming materials were available so his body was packed in salt for shipment to his home in Lancaster. Unidentified Federal dead were reinterred from their temporary graves and sent to the new National Cemetery. By the middle of November less than 100 patients remained and the camp was no longer required. Today only a single marker tells the story of the scene of so much pain and suffering. The Giant Supermarket and parking lot sit where Camp Letterman cared for the wounded from the greatest battle on the North American Continent.

The aftermath of the battle was horrid beyond any description. Over 7,000 bodies of the dead and dying littered the field. Burial fell to the Union troops or citizens of the area. Priority went to Federal dead and the Union soldiers buried as many as possible in shallow graves before they began the pursuit of the retreating Rebels southward. Burial for the northern dead was in shallow hand dug, individual graves with wooden markers where the names would be inscribed to aid in future re burial. Confederates were buried in trenches that would hold multiple bodies with no effort being made to preserve identification of the bodies. By the time removal of southern bodies began around 7 years after the war, identification of Southern dead would be next to impossible. Since all the graves were dug by hand, they were shallow and only gave minimal cover. For years after the war, bones and body parts would be uncovered by heavy rains or farmers plowing their fields. Far too many bodies were not buried and the corpses were left to rot in the hot sun.

Adding to the carnage was the mangled bodies of horses that were killed in action. As many as 5,000 horses were killed during the 3 days of fighting. Most of the animals were drenched in kerosene and burned, the smoke and odor adding to the macabre landscape. The skeletal remains would be utilized as fertilizer.

Citizens from outside the area flocked to Gettysburg after the battle. Many attempted to find the bodies of loved ones lost in the battle. Others came to the area to view the horrors of war first hand. Some of them came to collect souvenirs of the great battle. The Federal officials posted signs that the scattered accoutrements of war were government property and anyone caught with them would be arrested. Those that ignored the signs were arrested and forced to work on burial details as punishment.

The landscape was littered with discarded military equipment. Unfired muskets lay on the ground awaiting someone to unload the dangerous weapons. Unused cartridges were everywhere. The most dangerous were the artillery rounds that had failed to explode either due to faulty fuses or errors on the part of the gunners. More than one farmer was injured as he attempted to plow his field and detonated the unexploded shells. No attempt was made by the Army to disarm loaded projectiles. On Sunday July 5· two young souvenir hunters found an abandoned rifle in good condition. The older of the pair accidently fired the rifle making 3 year old Edward Woods the youngest person to die as a result of the battle.

In spite of all the fighting that took place within the town limits, only a single civilian casualty took place as a direct result of the battle. Twenty year old Jennie Wade was preparing dough to make biscuits in the McClellan house about mid way up Cemetery Hill along Baltimore Street. A stray sharpshooters' bullet passed through both doors of the house and struck her in the middle of her back, killing her instantly. She was engaged to marry Corporal "Jack" Skelly who was mortally wounded at the Battle of Winchester in June but the casualty list had not reached Gettysburg. Neither ever learned of the others death. The Jenny Wade House is famous for paranormal activity and is frequently visited by ghost tours.

The gate house of the Evergreen Cemetery at the time of the battle was the Peter Thorn residence. Peter was serving with the 138th PA Infantry but his wife Elizabeth lived in the gatehouse and cared for the cemetery before the battle. When Elizabeth, age 31 and pregnant returned on July 3 the area of the cemetery was littered with the dead. She buried 105 soldiers in the Evergreen Cemetery, Union and Confederate side by side in death. The gatehouse also served as a hospital and Elizabeth said it took four days of washing to get the blood out of the family's bedclothes.

The Union dead were hurriedly buried in inadequate graves. With the support of Pennsylvania Governor Andrew Curtin, property was purchased adjacent to the Evergreen Cemetery on Cemetery Hill to provide a permanent resting place for the fallen Federal troops. Dedicated on November 19, 1863 the Soldiers' National Cemetery at Gettysburg was the site of President Lincoln's famous address. By March of 1864, almost 3,500 Federal troops were reinterred in the new Cemetery.

It was not until 1870 that upon the initiative of the Southern Ladies Memorial associations, 3,320 Confederate bodies were relocated to grave sites below the Mason Dixon Line. The relocation of bodies took over 3 years with 2,935 bodies of the fallen being buried at the Hollywood Cemetery in Richmond. Most of the remains were unidentified after being in the ground for 7 years. It is widely believed that many of the remains were never relocated accounting for some of the spiritual activity in the area.

Residents that lived in the area returned to find their properties devastated by the fighting. John Rose, who owned the property where the worst of the fighting took place on the second day, found the graves of over 500 soldiers surrounding his home as well as another 1,500 in his woods. His crops were destroyed, livestock killed, fences knocked down and the peach trees in the orchard where the Third Corps was defeated were cut down and blown apart by confederate artillery. His house and barn were used as a field hospital and amputated limbs were stacked outside. Financial ruin would follow for the once prosperous farmer. His daughter would go insane from the horror of watching the removal of Confederate dead for reburial in the South following the war.

The William Bliss family owned a sixty acre farm west of the Emmitsburg Pike that had the unfortunate fate of lying between the two armies on the second day. The family wisely fled in such a hurry that they left the beds made and the table set. As the battle progressed, Connecticut infantry burned the house and barn to prevent the Confederates from using the buildings for cover. The only items saved momentarily were the Bliss chickens that the hungry Yankees took along as they fled the burning structures.

Today, the Lightner Farm House is a beautiful bed and breakfast where customers come to enjoy the peace and tranquility of the Pennsylvania country side. In 1863 Isaac Lightner was the Adams County sheriff and had built a brick Federal-style house on 19 acres. In anticipation of constructing a porch, the sheriff had stockpiled lumber for the project. Located within the Union lines, the house was confiscated for use as a field hospital by army surgeons. The farm was used primarily as a medical facility for the First Corps soldiers that absorbed the brunt of the attack on the first day. When Isaac Lightner returned to his house after the fighting of July 2, he found his home and property was being used as a field hospital with surgeons working in what is now the living and dining room. His family was delegated to living in the barn. After the battle ended and the wounded soldiers were removed from the house, the Lightners attempted to move back into their home. The stench was so horrible that they could not live there again and had to move to another location. His lumber was confiscated and used to make beds, operating tables and tent floors. Needless to say, the Lightner Farm House is a source of paranormal activity and ghost tours are conducted on a regular basis.

For Union prisoners of war, the nightmare of confinement in many instances produced a higher death rate than the battle itself. At Andersonville Prison, during a period of 2 months, records show that an average of 127 persons died each day. Many died from malnutrition or disease, but hundreds of others were shot when they crossed a clearly marked deadline. That meant that a body was pitched into an unmarked grave at a rate of one every 11 minutes.

Confederate prisoners did not fare any better in Northern prisons. An early tabulation shows more than 9,000 Confederates buried in cemeteries above the Mason Dixon Line. A small graveyard near the Alton, Illinois prison holds 662 unidentified bodies of Rebel soldiers.

Abraham Bryan was a free black that raised his family on a small farm that was located on Cemetery Ridge near Zigler's Grove. Unfortunately for the Bryan family, the house was situated on the edge of Pickett's Charge. When word of the Rebel troops moving northward arrived in Gettysburg, Bryan fled to avoid being returned to slavery south of the Mason Dixon line. The free black returned to find his house and barn destroyed by musket and artillery fire. He filed a claim with the Government to rebuild his home but received little in actual remuneration. His house and barn have been rebuilt by the National Park Service to its pre war condition.

General Robert E. Lee saw his Army of Northern Virginia heavily damaged by the Federal troops at Gettysburg with many of his best commanders either killed or wounded. His retreat to the relative safety of Virginia was long and difficult under the harassing eyes and guns of Northern Cavalry. Upon reaching the safety of the south, he submitted his resignation to President Jefferson Davis who promptly refused to accept it. The Confederacy would face two more years of punishing warfare. Lee suffered from degenerative heart disease and died in 1870.

Jefferson Davis, the only President of the Confederate States of America, was captured by the military while trying to escape through the deep south. He served two years in jail and was pardoned without a trial. He was stripped of his citizenship and died in 1889 a man without a country. His citizenship was restored during the administration of Jimmy Carter.

Lee's opponent at Gettysburg, General George Meade remained as commander of the Army of the Potomac until the Southern surrender at Appomattox. President Lincoln was angered that Meade did not pursue a counterattack at Gettysburg or an aggressive pursuit of the retreating Rebels. When Meade learned of Lincoln's anger he offered his resignation but it was refused because the President feared public backlash with the election only a year in the future. Even though Meade had delivered the first major victory for the Union, he was passed over for promotion as his subordinates were elevated in command. He became progressively bitter and passed away an angry man in 1872.

General Meade was quite devoted to his horse throughout the war. Named "Baldy" because of a patch of white on his head, the animal was wounded 14 times including a bullet that passed through the trouser leg of Meade and went into the animal's stomach at Gettysburg. After the horse recovered, Meade rode him through the campaigns of 1864 and finally retired the animal to a farm in Philadelphia. Baldy outlived Meade by 10 years and had to be euthanized at the age of 30 when he became too weak to stand because of old age.

J.E.B. Stuart, the swashbuckling commander of Confederate Cavalry performed admirably defending the retreating Southern forces. He spent the rest of his career attempting to defend his reputation from the lack of reconnaissance prior to the Battle of Gettysburg. The cavalry commander was mortally wounded in May 1864 at the Battle of Yellow Tavern near Richmond, VA. Historians still hotly debate whether his 10 day raid suffered from bad luck or poor command decisions. General Lee cried openly when he was informed of the death of Stuart and made the statement that Stuart had never given him a bad bit of information. He did not mention that his lack of information cost the Confederacy dearly at Gettysburg.

John Buford, the cavalry commander that committed the Union to fighting from the favorable ground of Gettysburg and held his position until reinforcements arrived, continued in active service. In the Fall of 1863 he contracted typhoid fever and died before the year ended. He is buried at West Point. The hard fighting Buford was one of the true heroes of the battle.

Confederate General James Longstreet continued as commander of the First Corps until the end of the war. He was badly wounded in the Wilderness in 1864 and rejoined the Army a few months before Appomattox. Longstreet was attacked in the press for his performance at Gettysburg because of supposed delay in positioning his troops on July 2 and his half hearted support of the grand assault. He published multiple articles criticizing General Lee and angered many southerners. There are not many monuments honoring Longstreet in the South. The general passed away in 1904.

Joshua Chamberlain, hero of Little Round Top as defender of the Union right flank, was wounded 6 times during the war. One of the wounds suffered during the Overland Campaign was so serious he was promoted to General because the Commander, General Grant, thought Chamberlain was on his death bed. Chamberlain survived to become Maine's first postwar Governor and would finish his life as president of Bowdoin College. He lectured and wrote extensively of the Civil War until his death in 1914. The exploits of Chamberlain and the 20th Maine became famous when their role at Gettysburg was detailed in Michael Shaara's book "Killer Angels" and became a major part of the movie "Gettysburg" in 1994.

Confederate General Henry Heth was in charge of the troops that that made first contact and committed his forces to battle in spite of General Lee's orders not to engage in any contact with the enemy. Heth is probably best known for making up the excuse that his troops were seeking shoes in Gettysburg as a reason for not obeying Lee's orders. It seemed like a good excuse at the time but in reality there were no shoe factories in Gettysburg. Heth was wounded in the head at Gettysburg but was wearing a hat that was too large and was stuffed with paper. The paper deflected the bullet but he was knocked unconscious, keeping him from making any more stupid decisions during the battle. He died in 1899 after becoming an insurance salesman.

The small town of Gettysburg was changed forever. Visitors flocked to the area to observe the site of the turning point of the War of the Rebellion (or as my Southern friends call it, the War of Northern Agression). Federal veterans that survived the fighting raised money and erected monuments in the locations where they were engaged. Monuments to Confederates were discouraged by the Grand Army of the Republic and early land acquisition focused on preserving positions held by the North. Much of the land held by Rebel troops has been lost to development. For instance, Gettysburg High School was built on land used in the Confederate assault on East Cemetery Hill and a monument stands along the edge of their running track.

Tourist exploitation has been taking place almost since the sound of the gunfire ended. The Gettysburg and Harrisburg Railroad built a spur in 1884 that ran across portions of Pickett's Charge to the Slaughter Pen area. The railroad established a 13 acre park at the base of Little Round Top, complete with pavilions, a photography studio, a dance hall and kitchen. A casino was added to the Park in 1913. The tracks and dance hall were removed in 1939. History has a way of repeating itself.

It was not until 1895 that President Grover Cleveland established the Gettysburg National Military Park consisting of about 800 acres and 300 monuments at the time. Today there are over 1,600 monuments and markers in the 6,000 acres maintained by the National Park Service. In 1933, the 70th anniversary of the fighting, President Franklin Delano Roosevelt dedicated the Eternal Light on Oak Hill where Rebel artillery battered Union positions on the first day of battle. Almost 2 million visitors a year tour the Park today. There is no way to tell how many spirits still haunt the area.

Perhaps the greatest aftermath of the Battle of Gettysburg is the spiritual presence that continues to haunt the 25 plus square miles that history remembers as the turning point of the Civil War. As I have demonstrated in this book, their presence is shown in varied ways from residual to intelligent haunting. Hopefully I have treated the presence of those who fought on this hallowed ground with respect and honor, for they all paid dearly with their last breath near the town of Gettysburg.

Suggested Reading

Adelman, G. (2000). *Little Round Top: A Detailed Guide*. Gettysburg, PA: Thomas Publications.

Adelman G. & Smith T. (1997) *Devil's Den: A History & Guide*. Gettysburg, PA: Thomas Publications.

Boritt, G. S. (1997). *The Gettysburg Nobody Knows*. Oxford, NY: Oxford University Press.

Busenitz, J. (n.d.). *6th Wisconsin at Gettysburg*. Retrieved from Military History Online: www.militaryhistoryonline.com/gettysburg

Coco, G. A. (1995). *A Strange and Blighted Land. Gettysburg: The Aftermath of a Battle*. Gettysburg, PA: Thomas Publications.

Elliott, S. (n.d.). *Elliott's Map of the Battlefield of Gettysburg*. Library of Congress Geography and Map Division. Washington, D.C.

Garrison, W. (1994). *Civil War Curiosities*. Nashville, TN: Rutledge Hill Press.

Gindlesperger, J. A. (2010). *So You Think You Know Gettysburg*. Winston Salem, NC: John F. Blair.

Gottfreid, B. M. (2008). *The Artillery of Gettysburg*. Nashville, TN: Cumberland House.

Heiser, J. G. (n.d.). *The Battle of Gettysburg in Detal*. Retrieved from National Park Service: www.nps.gov/archive

Jorgensen, J. (2002). *The Wheatfield at Gettysburg: A Walking Tour*. Gettysburg, PA: Thomas Publications.

Krick, R. &. (2004). *The Gettysburg Death Roster*. Dayton, OH: Morningside Bookshop.

Longacre, E. G. (1993). *The Cavalry at Gettysburg*. Lincoln, NB: University of Nevada Press.

Longstreet, J. (1896, Reprint 1984). *From Manassass to Appomaattox*. Secaucus, NJ: Blue and Gray Press.

McAulay, J. D. (1981). *Carbines of the Civil War*. Union City, TN: Pioneer Press.

McAulay, J. D. (1987). *Civil War Breech Loading Rifles*. Lincoln, Rhode Island: Andrew Mobray Inc.

McCellan, G. (1886). *McClellan's Own Story*. New York, NY.: Charles Webster & Co.

McClellan, H. (1993). *The Campaigns of Stuart's Cavalry.* Seacaucus, NJ: Blue and Gray Press.

McPherson, J. M. (2003). *Hallowed Ground.* New York, NY: Crown Publishers.

Stackpole, E. &. (1998). *Battle of Gettysburg, A Guided Tour.* Mechanicsburg, PA: Stackpole Books.

Swanberg, W. (1956). *Sickles the Incredible.* Charles Schribner's Sons: New York, NY.

Sword, W. (1988). *Sharpshooter: Hiram Berdan, his famous Sharpsshooters and their Sharps Rifles.* Lincoln, RI: Andrew Mowbray, Inc.

Teague, C. (n.d.). *Barlow's Knob Revisited.* Retrieved from Military History Online: www.militaryhistoryonline.com

Thomas, J. (2005). *The First Day at Gettysburg: A Walking Tour.* Gettysburg, PA: Thomas Publications.

Toney B. K. (2008) *Battlefield Ghosts.* Gettysburg, PA: Thomas Publications.

Trudeau, N. (2003). *Gettysburg, A Testing of Courage.* New York, NY: Perennial Publishing.

Unknown. (n.d.). *America's Most Haunted Places.* Retrieved from Prairie Ghosts: www.prarieghosts.com

Unknown. (1883). *Battles and Leaders of the Civil War, Vol. 3.* Seacacus, NJ: Castle.

Unknown. (n.d.). *Maps of Gettysburg, Pennsylvania (1863).* Retrieved from Civil War Trust: www.civilwar.org

Warner, E. J. (1986). *Generals in Blue.* Baton Rouge, LA: Louisiana University Press.

Warner, E. J. (1986). *Generals in Gray.* Baton Rouge, LA: Louisiana University Press.

About the Author

Barry Strohm was born near Hershey, Pennsylvania, but is currently a resident of Park City, Utah. There he resides with his wife of 46 years, Connie. The owner of the Golden Lane Art and Antique Gallery in New Oxford, PA, for 22 years, the author has become familiar with the spirit world because of the events that happen at the Gallery. Lights turn on when on one is around and footsteps are heard when the store is empty. Professional investigations have proven that the Golden Lane Gallery is one of the most haunted buildings in the country. Since New Oxford is only nine miles from the Gettysburg battlefield, it seemed obvious that pursuit of the paranormal where so many died would yield spectacular results.

What started as a casual interest in paranormal photography turned into an obsession as the author spent evenings in the dark taking over 50,000 pictures in a three-year span. Friends looking at these pictures kept saying, "you should write a book." Their statements have become a reality; the author hopes you are pleased with the results.